BECAUSE
YOU MATTER

BECAUSE
YOU MATTER

HOW TO TAKE OWNERSHIP OF YOUR
LIFE SO YOU CAN REALLY LIVE

DANIELLE BERNOCK

Copyright © Danielle Bernock 2019 All rights reserved

This book is designed to provide information and motivation to the reader. The ideas and suggestions in this book are not intended as a substitute for consulting with licensed professionals. It is sold with the understanding that the publisher is not engaged to render any type of psychological, legal, or any other kind of professional advice. Neither the author nor the publisher shall be liable or responsible for any loss, injury, or damage allegedly arising from any information or suggestion in this book. Our views and rights are the same: You are responsible for your own choices, actions, and results. References are provided for informational purposes only and readers should be aware that the websites listed in this book may change.

Edited by Karlene Jacobsen

Interior photos© Danielle Bernock

Text from definitions.net Copyright 2019, STANDS4 LLC. All rights reserved. Used by permission.

Unless otherwise identified, scripture references and quotations are from the King James Version of the Bible. Public domain. Scripture quotations marked NIV are taken from THE HOLY BIBLE, NEW INTERNATIONAL VERSION®, NIV® Copyright © 1973, 1978, 1984, 2011 by Biblica, Inc.® Used by permission. All rights reserved worldwide. Scripture quotations marked ERV are taken from the HOLY BIBLE: EASY-TO-READ VERSION © 2001 by World Bible Translation Center, Inc. and used by permission. Scripture quotations marked NKJV are taken from the New King James Version®. Copyright © 1982 by Thomas Nelson. Used by permission. All rights reserved. Scripture quotations marked TLB are taken from The Living Bible copyright © 1971. Used by permission of Tyndale House Publishers, Inc., Carol Stream, Illinois 60188. All rights reserved. Scripture quotations marked GW are taken from GOD'S WORD®, © 1995 God's Word to the Nations. Used by permission of Baker Publishing Group. Scripture quotations marked NLT are taken from the Holy Bible, New Living Translation, copyright © 1996, 2004, 2015 by Tyndale House Foundation. Used by permission of Tyndale House Publishers, Inc., Carol Stream, Illinois 60188. All rights reserved. Scripture quotations marked GNT are from the Good News Bible© 1994 published by the Bible Societies/HarperCollins Publishers Ltd UK, Good News Bible© American Bible Society 1966, 1971, 1976, 1992. Used with permission. Scripture quotations marked MSG are taken from The Message. Copyright © 1993, 1994, 1995, 1996, 2000, 2001, 2002. Used by permission of NavPress Publishing Group.

Author website: https://www.daniellebernock.com

ISBN 978-0-9961033-3-6

4F Media *"Faith Family Friends Freedom"*

P.O. Box 183203, Shelby Township, MI 48317

First Printing 2019

*To the wounded heart,
fighting for freedom,
with tears streaming down your face:
you are a warrior.*

Table of Contents

Endorsements ... ix
Acknowledgments ... xiii
Note to Reader ... xvii

1. Why This Book ... 1
2. Why Ownership ... 13
3. Owning Your Choices ... 21
    How Jackie Took Ownership of Her Life ... 33
4. Owning Your Value ... 39
    How John Took Ownership of His Life ... 52
5. Owning Your Courage ... 59
    How Sylvia Took Ownership Of Her Life ... 73
6. Owning Your Mess ... 79
    How Randy Took Ownership Of His Life ... 92
7. Owning Your Pain ... 99
    How Nancy Took Ownership Of Her Life ... 115
8. Owning Your Emotions ... 121
    How Andre Took Ownership Of His Life ... 142
9. Owning Your Mind ... 147
    How Mary Took Ownership Of Her Life ... 166
10. Owning Grace ... 171
    How Tom Took Ownership Of His Life ... 183

11. Owning Your Process	191
How Naomi Took Ownership Of Her Life	213
12. Owning Your Wholeness	219
How Jeff Took Ownership Of His Life	234
13. Owning Your Purpose	241
More from the Author	251
Endnotes	253
References	263

Endorsements

"We all experience trauma. *Because You Matter* helps bring you to the other side of it, where you can embrace the joy of life again. This book is for every wounded person searching to be free from pain, shame, and the feelings of worthlessness we all face."

JEFF GOINS

Bestselling Author of *The Art of Work*

"I have been following Danielle Bernock's work for over a year now, and I am always inspired by her ability to see situations and challenges in a new way. She is uplifting and her focus is on appreciating your own unique life—the good and the bad. This book is a compilation of wisdom from Danielle and others she has interviewed (some famous, some not), but all offer the opportunity to view your own life through new eyes."

SANDY PECKINPAH

Author of *How to Survive the Worst that Can Happen*

"Want to know you matter? This book will show you the way. Rather than rehash what you've already heard, Danielle Bernock takes you on a deep dive to discover your value. Get this book today and start living the life you were made for."

FRANK MCKINLEY

Bestselling Author of *10 Steps to Effective Leadership*

"Danielle Bernock's earnestness shines through on every page. *Because You Matter* would fit well on a shelf of Christian devotionals, but there are gems in here that even non-Christians such as myself can appreciate."

MELISSA DINWIDDIE

Author of *The Creative Sandbox Way™: Your Path to a Full-Color Life.*

"In BECAUSE YOU MATTER, Danielle has given us more than a self-help manual. She has invited us on a journey to experience true healing and wholeness. Her transparency is refreshing and beckons us to allow God to bring us to the place of our true identity. I love this book, and that's why I highly recommend it!"

S. J. HILL

Author of *Enjoying God, A Love For The Ages*, And *What's God Really Like?*

"*'They overcame him* (Satan) *by the blood of the lamb, and by the word of their testimony.'* I am so proud of Danielle for sharing hope with others through her testimony and journey to healing and wholeness. As a trauma coach and leader of a nonprofit helping victims, I'm thrilled to have this new book available as a resource to help those who've been wounded."

PAULA MOSHER WALLACE

Founder and President of *Bloom in the Dark Inc.*, Producer, and Cohost of *Bloom Today Television Show*, Managing Partner of *Fertilizer Films*, and Producer and Creator of *Recovery Strategies 4 Life.*

ENDORSEMENTS

"Danielle's book weaves inspiration, scripture, and real-life stories of hope to encourage you to believe in yourself, your dreams, and the difference you can make in the world—*Because You Matter!*"

LISA ROBBIN YOUNG

Founder, *Ark Entertainment Media*, LisaRobbinYoung.com

Acknowledgments

To write this section of the book, I reviewed the one in my first book. I realized I needed to acknowledge that first book, or perhaps my *"journey to emerge."* It might sound strange because it's not a person, and traditionally, that's what you read in this section. But when I released it, I had no idea I'd be where I am today. That I'd be helping so many others on their *"journey to emerge,"* and then take flight after processing their growth. So, if you had any part in *Emerging With Wings,* your name belongs in this section. Thank you for helping me become my true self.

Next, I need to thank all the people who were touched by that first book and communicated it to me. Knowing my words brought life to you compelled me to market my book so I could reach more people. I began researching how to do that. This book exists because you spoke up.

A hearty thank you to Adam S. McHugh (author of *The Listening Life*) for his article *Promoting a Book in 10 Painfully Easy Steps*. Your words *"each book needs a blog"* stuck in my soul like burrs on a collie's belly after a romp through the field. I needed a blog and returned to an old one I'd started on a free platform. I utilized every free resource I could find endeavoring to follow your advice. It got hard, and I wanted to quit many times, but I couldn't shake those five words of yours. Somehow, I knew you were right. If I would've quit, this book wouldn't exist.

Thank you, Jeff Goins (founder of Tribe Writers). To follow Adam's advice, I devoured your free tools and resources about writing, finding your audience, and the technical things about blogging. Soon after, I became a member of your Tribe Writers and have never looked back. What you created with Tribe Writers is not only a paid course but a community of writers which has been invaluable. You made me understand the value of community, and I've become a different person.

This leads me to all my writer friends. Tribe Writers, Tribe Builders Network, Rochester Writers, Creative Writers Workshop, and others not in those groups. I can't possibly list you all by name. Your encouragement and support are beyond words. I love you guys so much.

To my Beta Readers: Your kind encouragement and corrections changed many things in this book. One thing you wanted was more stories, and as I looked for ways to give you what you wanted, the interview idea came to deliver them. You are precious souls to look at a writer's first usable draft and give honest feedback. I can't thank you enough.

Thank you, Jackie, John, Sylvia, Randy, Nancy, Andre, Mary, Tom, Naomi, and Jeff, for giving your precious time, sharing your amazing stories, and blessing my heart. Naomi, my daughter, thank you for telling me about that book with the stories between chapters, being my first guinea pig interview, and then letting me interview you again so I could record it. Jeff, thank you for being a good friend, supporter, inspiration, and courageously sharing things about your life you never had before. Randy, thank you for your prayers and encouragement, and for going to those emotionally hard places again to help others. John, thank you for all you do to help the traumatized heal, and for helping me see why you're so strong. Nancy, thank you for your gracious courage and tenacity—you're a walking inspiration. Andre, thank you for being such an amazing example of how knowing your value makes all the difference in life and allowing me to be a part of your journey. Tom, thank you for overcoming so much and sharing your gifts, talents, and victories with the world, and for spreading your positivity everywhere. Mary, thank you for sharing your expertise as my media coach, and for the honor of calling you a friend. Sylvia, thank you for letting me interview you when I'd only met you once, all the tears and laughter we shared and telling me your story about peas—I will never look at peas the same again.

My precious friend, Cheryl, you've walked with me through this whole process. When I got discouraged, you encouraged me. When I needed support and prayer, you were there. You always asked how things were going and let me ramble on and on. Your genuine interest in the mission of this book touches my heart deeply. I love you dearly and thank God for you.

My beloved family. Thank you for your support throughout this long process and caring about my mission, especially my husband, Michael. You've been my greatest cheerleader, encourager, supporter and promoter. I wouldn't be here today without you. I love you all beyond words.

Finally, this wouldn't be complete without my greatest love. The one who pursued me when I was running in fear and pain. The one who patiently and graciously ushered me past every trauma into a place of loving freedom that I didn't know existed. My God who loves me with an everlasting love: I love you because you loved me first. I am eternally grateful.

Note to Reader

This book is a work of love to empower you in life. When I began writing this for you, I used my story alone to help reclaim your life from childhood/emotional trauma. Having fought for my own healing and freedom, I'm compelled to help others gain what I've found. However, my story alone isn't enough. You deserve more.

I'm certain there are things from my life that *will* help you. But not everything will because we're all different. To enlarge your experience and provide you with more tools, I've included the wisdom and stories from others.

In these pages, you'll find 100 quotes from various people. Some are famous, some are not, and the ones without last names are people from the Bible. I've compiled them separately in a PDF for you, free upon request as a thank you for purchasing my book.

I've also gathered stories through the interviews of ten amazing people: men and women, black and white, Millennials to Baby Boomers, with varying applications of faith. Taking ownership of what you believe is one thing I touch on this book—because everyone believes something. I am a Christian, but maybe you're not. I respect what you choose to believe.

At the close of each chapter are key points, an optional prayer, and a place for notes. Between each *Owning* chapter are the stories from my interviews. You'll find more information about each person and what they have to offer in the *Endnotes*.

As you go through this book, take what works for you, and set aside the rest. More than anything else, I desire you will fully own your life. It's yours, and it's your right to do so.

I wish you freedom,

Danielle

danielleberrnock.com
dani@danielleberrnock.com

CHAPTER 1

Why This Book

Only I can change my life. No one can do it for me.

—Carol Burnett

My dear reader, you've been given one life, and it can be amazing if you take ownership of it. Life is more than performing daily tasks and subtracting bad days from good days. Your life is worth more than enduring hard seasons, hoping for better ones and suffering trauma.

When Jesus told his disciples, *"In this world you will have trouble,"* He wasn't delivering a mandate, or providing an excuse to live in constant trouble or misery. Murphy's law (anything that can go wrong will go wrong) isn't a law. It's a negative state of mind that'll rob your life of joy. You don't have to live that way. Jesus also said, *"I am come that they might have life, and that they might have it more abundantly."* More abundantly. Not just abundantly, but *more*! You can experience this abundance, but it's not automatic. Jesus also said *might*. There isn't a guarantee. It requires owning it.

Look at your life. This one life you get to live. How's it going? Are you happy, content, satisfied? Living the dream? Or are you struggling, disappointed, emotionally tired, disillusioned? Are you dealing with shame, chronic pain, frustration, feeling miserable? Do you wonder when it's going to get easier? When are things going to go your way?

I have good news for you. You can change your life—if you want to.

The key is in your hand.

YOUR LIFE MATTERS

Loving your life because it's precious to God honors Him.
—Danielle Bernock

Owning your life is how you'll find joy, power, satisfaction, and even salvation. Yes, salvation. Not just the eternal when you die kind of salvation. But the here and now preserving of who you are. The real you. The true you. The precious eternal soul God created you to be. God loves your soul and wants you to love it too.

This book will challenge your thinking. Don't let that scare you. Growth requires both learning and unlearning. When you're done reading, you'll feel emancipated; you'll know how to break free of life-sucking condemnation, soul pain, and perpetual misery.

Are you ready to reclaim the life you were born to live?

IT'S A JOURNEY

A year from now you will wish you had started today.

—Karen Lamb

This journey isn't easy or fast. You didn't get where you are now in a moment, and becoming your true "whole" self isn't a work of magic. This process will be extensive, but worth everything you have.

I began my journey, unaware of how the term ownership applied to my life. In 2014, I released my first book, *Emerging With Wings,* to the world. I took a step in vulnerability I'd never taken before. It was both exhilarating and terrifying. Shame held me captive, causing me to hide most of my life. Sharing my story—warts and all—made me feel like I stripped off all my clothes and ran around the world naked. The way people responded shocked me. I touched them far deeper than I dared to hope. The positive reviews, texts, and emails were astounding. Discovering my book—*my story*—was being used in a sermon boggled my mind.

Not long after, I learned how fragile my new understanding was when asked to speak to a group of women. Instead of accepting the offer, I recoiled in fear. The lost moment and my fearful response plagued me. *Why wasn't I able to accept this amazing opportunity? Isn't this why I shared my story? If I had emerged with wings as my book said, then this wouldn't be happening. What was wrong with me? I thought I was different.* I was. What these questions revealed was a need for more growth.

Enter the story of a newly emerged butterfly[1] and how it relates to our lives.

LEARNING FROM THE BUTTERFLY

You must want to fly so much that you are willing to give up being a caterpillar.

—Trina Paulus

My first book is a journey of becoming free from childhood trauma and finding my value. I compared my transformation to a caterpillar changing into a butterfly and emerging from its chrysalis. The imagery stood! When I published my story, I *did* emerge. What I wrote *was* true. I *was* different. A transformation *had* occurred. I was no longer who I was before. I was in a new place with wrong information. I thought newly emerged butterflies just flew away. They don't. The new me was like a newly emerged butterfly. When a butterfly emerges, it's completely intact but unable to fly. It has a process it must complete, or it will never fly. How does a butterfly truly live if it never flies? It doesn't.

The wings of a new butterfly are weak and wet. They must be prepared for flight.

- They need to hang upside down with plenty of room for their wings to expand.
- They need to pump blood (hemolymph) into the veins in their wings so they can expand to their full size.
- Their wings must dry.
- They must exercise their flight muscles. (I didn't know butterflies had muscles, did you?)
- Finally, the butterfly must expel meconium (poop) which is the waste remains of its last meal from when it was a caterpillar.

During this process, the new butterfly looks like it's doing nothing, but it's quite busy. Likewise, when I emerged, I couldn't fly. I needed to prepare my proverbial wings. During my writing process, multiple transformative things occurred. Revelations, realizations, and courage to become vulnerable. I went through the publishing process, and still, the fear was there. On the day I released it, I was not fit to fly. I needed to do several things:

- Own this new life like a butterfly prepares its wings.
- Give myself the time to see from this new perspective and let these new things sink in like the butterfly hangs upside down.
- Give myself the grace and space I need for this new process like the butterfly needs room to expand.
- Build new mindsets like the butterfly pumps blood into its wings.
- Solidify my new beliefs like the butterfly exercises its muscles.
- And like the butterfly needs to poop before it can fly, I needed to get rid of some crap in my life.

Only after doing so could I move on to learn and become skilled in using my new wings.

DANGER

A masterpiece does not unfurl its wings immediately. It takes time. It will fly when it is ready.

—A.D. Posey

It's in this part of a butterfly's life it's most vulnerable to predators because it can't fly away. I was in a place of danger and didn't understand. Until it happened—an epic meltdown that changed my life.

But let's back up.

The year following the release, and re-release, of my first book, was full of intensity. Extremes in both circumstances and emotions. Happy vs. sad. Joy vs. sorrow. Elation vs. grief. There was a lot of pressure. My husband worked out of town most of the year, trusting me with the oversight of his mother's care, who suffered from Alzheimer's. I didn't notice my personal storm properly within this family one. I knew I was having mini-meltdowns here and there. My relationship with wine grew close. But I was focused on keeping one foot in front of the other.

During this time, I put enormous pressure on myself to do, and be, all my family needed. I expected strong wings. I'd emerged. I demanded much of myself, but my wings were wet, and I still had crap. It took that epic meltdown to open my eyes.

The journey of taking ownership of one's life is long. Lifelong. Yes, you make progress, like I did, but if your objective is to read this book and find a magic wand to happiness, you've got the wrong book. On the other hand, if you're tired of being miserable and ready to do something about it so you can enjoy this life you've been given, find fulfillment and come to the end of it without regret, this is the book for you.

Let me warn you, though. If you don't allow yourself to heal and grow, you won't really live. In fact, if you don't, that life-sucking condemnation and soul pain will steal your life away. Consequently, you run the risk of leaving this life a bitter and fearful soul before your time. Please don't.

THE DARE

Resistance to change is as powerful as resistance to creative effort
—Tim Grahl

I dare you to take ownership of your life—who you are and who you want to be. Why dare? Because our humanity kicks against being *told* what to do. But when we're challenged, we are more likely to respond with the attitude: *watch me!* I hope you'll choose the latter response because it'll serve you on your journey.

I didn't understand I had the power to own anything in my life due to childhood trauma and lack of knowledge. Trauma creates soul wounds that leave a person feeling powerless. Loss of power strips a person of their sense of value. If you've suffered childhood trauma, I dare you to believe you can be healed and free. I did, and I believe you can too.

Emotional trauma in adulthood also strips value and power. This book is about reclaiming your power and value. It's about allowing yourself to be loved into wholeness. Humans are complex beings, so there are numerous things to address. I dare you to own all that rightfully belongs to you.

BECAUSE YOU MATTER

Loving and owning our lives is how we become whole, one piece of truth at a time.

—Danielle Bernock

In this book, we'll go deep. Deep into your value and where it comes from. Your power and what it's for. How these things are owned and what they produce.

We'll talk about *why* you matter. Owning who you are right now and who you want to become. We'll discuss owning your courage, your choices, your right to be loved, your mindsets, your responses, your growth, and more.

Because You Matter.

THERE'S A LOT TO LEARN AND A LIFETIME TO DO IT

But by the grace of God I am what I am, and his grace to me was not without effect

—Paul

When I started writing my first book, I knew I had a lot to share. I didn't know how much more I'd discover. I'm here now, with more to share. This time, however, I know there's much more to learn. Learning taught me the value of learning. For example, a while back, I started writing another book. I'd gathered valuable lessons and wanted to help people. I've learned many things the hard way. Sometimes due to stubbornness, and other times to lack of information and tools. I soon realized I wasn't ready to write another book. I had to grow more. My wings weren't strong enough, yet.

I took writing courses and joined a group called Tribe Writers to learn about writing and how to get my message to my audience. When I published my first book, this wasn't the case. Instead, I was afraid. When it came time to publish, my greatest fear was someone would actually read it. Many someones have. It was through the process of sharing my messy life and seeing how it changed the lives of others that I realized my need to let go of the fear. In my first book, I shared deeply embarrassing and emotionally intimate parts of my life. I discovered those are the things people need. They connect us.

Looking back, I can see when I started writing that second book, I was holding back, covering for self-protection. I had to stop hiding and live in the light, even when others might not like it, disagree, or judge me. I know so much more than I did before; and yet, so little compared to what there is to be known. My wings are ready now.

BOTTOM LINE

Because in our pain we must find each other—mirror to mirror the grace of our shared humanity, the stunningly broken beauty of our shared grief. And you can let your grief see my grief and let our tears mingle into some kind of healing alchemy, and you'll know what I know. That we are never alone. I promise. You and me? We are never, ever alone.

—Jeanette LeBlanc

This book exists because God wants you to know how much you're loved—how much you matter. He wants you to heal, to grow, and embrace the abundant life designed for you. The title of this book was whispered to my heart by the Spirit of Grace, commissioning this message for you.

Love said it best: Because you matter.

KEY POINTS

- You have only one life to live, and it's up to you how you live it.
- You can change your life if you want to.
- This journey isn't easy or fast.
- It takes space and grace to grow, and sometimes we have to get rid of some crap.
- You can enjoy life and find fulfillment.
- Every dare is designed to invoke a *"watch me"* attitude.
- This book exists because you matter.

YOU CAN ASK GOD FOR HELP

God help me. Taking ownership of my life sounds hard and scary. But I want to heal and grow. I want the abundant life Jesus came to give me. Help me learn and unlearn the things I need to. Help me accept your love and grace and embark on this journey to become my true self—the person You created me to be.

NOTES

CHAPTER 2

Why Ownership

It's your life, you get to decide what to do with it.

—Danielle Bernock

On the back of the brown wooden door to my room, I hid it beneath my bathrobe. I secretly hoped to own the positive qualities the poem offered: things like acceptance, encouragement, love, confidence, and security. But hiding it there gave me no ownership. Instead, I owned shame, judgment, criticism, and fear. I owned them even though I didn't understand ownership as a child. But the hidden poem became a prophecy as I learned what I lived.

Growing up, I understood responsibility. It was a duty and an obligation. I never considered owning my life. I didn't feel I had any right. Unless children are intentionally taught, they won't learn how to own their lives. This is exacerbated when trauma becomes part of a child's story. This happened to me which I'll get into more later. First, I want you to recognize the difference between responsibility and ownership.

Seeing the difference came as an *aha moment* for me. I read an article, illustrating the point of how different the two words were in a parenting situation. The word ownership haunted me long after I read about it. I researched both words to understand them better. Responsibility is a duty and obligation that has its place. But it can also be oppressive. This is due to a lack of ownership.

What's the difference?

Responsibility is *being* something.

Ownership is to *have* something.

Responsibility is a relationship between you and someone else. Ownership is a relationship with something that belongs to you.

When you're responsible for something, you answer to someone else. For example, when you rent or lease a vehicle. There are rules and requirements you're responsible for following. You must answer to the owner of the vehicle upon the end of your contract. If you've violated any of the guidelines or there's damage, you're responsible to the owner for those things.

When you own something, you answer only to yourself. Using the same example of a vehicle, this time you buy it. It belongs to you. You can choose to take care of it or not. It's up to you and you alone if you follow any manufacturer guidelines or not. You have the power to sell the vehicle to someone else if you want to.

Taking ownership of your life is better than taking ownership of things. It's empowering. Ownership inspires initiative, creativity, inventiveness, and resourcefulness. It's motivating. When you own something, you understand no one else has any responsibility unless you give it to them. When something is yours, you care more. Ownership is closer to our heart's affections than responsibility.

When, where, and to whom you were born were not in your power. You can't be held responsible for things outside your control. As you grew up, things happened that shaped who you are. Good and bad things. Things that weren't your fault and things that were. Maybe you suffered childhood trauma, as I did. Maybe you didn't. But either way, your life can change starting today by taking ownership of it going forward.

Childhood trauma has many causes. Some are obvious, while others are not. Consequently, trauma can go undetected. A child's brain isn't fully developed, so they aren't capable of handling things like adults. This means they're more susceptible to trauma. Things adults dismiss can inflict deep wounds in a child's psyche. A child can be traumatized and not understand the wounds embedded inside them. These wounds have voices that cry out for help. Sometimes this is why a child will "act out." When unheard and untended, the wounds cause symptoms (or side effects) in adults. We'll get more into what those are later. It's important to know the symptoms of childhood trauma will last a lifetime if not addressed. It was by the grace of God, and through His power, I found help and healing. You can too if that's what you need. God will help you if that's what you want.

GOD WANTS US TO TAKE OWNERSHIP FOR OUR LIVES

Something happens when you feel ownership. You no longer act like a spectator or consumer, because you're an owner. Faith is at its best when it's that way too. It's best lived when it's owned.

—Bob Goff

As a child, I never imagined God wanted me to own my life. There are religious views that consider it evil. I'm familiar with the Bible verses used in their argument because I oppressed myself with them until I learned better. I'm prepared to answer the objection for those who need it. Feel free to skip this section if this doesn't apply to you.

ADDRESSING THE ARGUMENT TO OWNERSHIP

Do you not know that your bodies are temples of the Holy Spirit, who is in you, whom you have received from God? You are not your own; you were bought at a price. Therefore, honor God with your bodies. (1 Cor. 6:19–20 NIV)

Now it is God who makes both us and you stand firm in Christ. He anointed us, set his seal of ownership on us, and put his Spirit in our hearts as a deposit, guaranteeing what is to come. (2 Cor. 1:21–22 NIV)

Do these verses say you have no rights? You're a slave to God? You're a robot and have no choices? Absolutely not. I misunderstood these for many years, thinking I was a slave and God a taskmaster. This is far from the truth. Now, I believe this way of thinking breaks God's heart.

The Bible says Jesus came to set us free. It's within freedom we're to take ownership of our lives and do something with them. We can't honor God with our body if we don't own it. Our body won't do it by itself. The Biblical seal of ownership is not one that turns us into another's property, like human trafficking. It's one of love and relationship. It's better compared to a betrothal with an engagement ring.

It is for freedom that Christ has set us free. Stand firm, then, and do not let yourselves be burdened again by a yoke of slavery. (Gal. 5:1 NIV)

You, my brothers and sisters, were called to be free. But do not use your freedom to indulge the flesh; rather, serve one another humbly in love. (Gal. 5:13 (NIV)

The freedom Christ purchased for us needs to be owned for us to walk in it. We won't love others without being intentional. We can oppress ourselves with certain behaviors burdened by the idea of responsibility; but, if we take ownership instead, it empowers us to live and love wholeheartedly. We'll sacrifice anything for true love. Look at what Jesus did.

What about dying to self and living for God? I'm glad you asked.

Then he said to them all: "Whoever wants to be my disciple must deny themselves and take up their cross daily and follow me. For whoever wants to save their life will lose it, but whoever loses their life for me will save it." (Luke 9:23-24 NIV)

Therefore, I urge you, brothers and sisters, in view of God's mercy, to offer your bodies as a living sacrifice, holy and pleasing to God—this is your true and proper worship. (Rom. 12:1 NIV)

". . . And I'll say to myself, "You have plenty of grain laid up for many years. Take life easy; eat, drink and be merry."' "But God said to him, 'You fool! This very night your life will be demanded from you. Then who will get what you have prepared for yourself?' "This is how it will be with whoever stores up things for themselves but is not rich toward God." (Luke 12:19-21 NIV)

The following definition of ownership explains how it's through taking ownership of our lives; we have the power to give them to God.

Ownership (noun) the relation of an owner to the thing possessed; possession **with the right to transfer possession to others**[2] (emphasis mine)

The Bible calls us joint-heirs with Jesus. In First Corinthians 6 (referenced above), the word own—*you're not your own*—has a long list of possible word translations in the original Greek[3]. One of them is *alone*. Try reading it instead as *you are not alone*. God has no interest in robots. The God I know desires relationship. He wants sons and daughters who will take ownership of, or "possess," what He's offered us. Our life, our soul, is a precious gift from God.

What good will it be for someone to gain the whole world, yet forfeit their soul? Or what can anyone give in exchange for their soul? (Matt. 16:26 NIV)

By your patience possess your souls. (Luke 21:19 NKJV)

The soul is made up of our mind, will, and emotions. These are three areas in our lives where we can take ownership. We'll talk more about these in separate chapters.

THE CHOICE IS UP TO YOU

Until you take ownership for your life, you will always be chasing happiness.

—Sean Stephenson

This life you're living is yours. It's up to you what you do with it. When it's over, you'll be left with the result of your choice. Taking ownership is being intentional within every area of your life and choosing to live it fully.

Is anything worth more than your soul? (Matt. 16:26b NLT)

Not only is our soul a gift from God. It's also our choice what we do with it.

KEY POINTS

- Taking ownership is more powerful than taking responsibility.
- Ownership is closer to our heart affections than responsibility.
- Whether you suffered childhood trauma like I did or not, your life can change starting today by taking ownership of it going forward.
- God wants you to take ownership of your life.
- The Biblical seal of ownership is one of love and relationship.
- It's through taking ownership of our lives we have the power to give them to God.
- Not only is our soul a gift from God. It's also our choice what we do with it.

YOU CAN ASK GOD FOR HELP

Father God, in Jesus name, I ask for your grace and power to help me take ownership of my life so I can live the life you have for me. Help me see things like you see them and not argue with your goodness.

NOTES

CHAPTER 3

Owning Your Choices

Trauma creates change you DON'T choose. Healing is about creating change you DO choose.

—Michele Rosenthal

HOW TO BEGIN

Taking ownership of one's life involves choices. Decisions made deliberately and intentionally. We make decisions every day, but sometimes we're unaware of them or their impact. We're going to talk about the decisions we *can* make to bring about the changes we *want* in our lives. As the quote above states, trauma creates changes we don't choose. This is true of childhood (developmental trauma). It's also true of emotional trauma in adults caused by death, divorce, job loss, or other tragedy. We can't change what's happened, but we have the power to choose how to proceed. There are countless choices in the process to heal, grow, and live the life we want to live. No day will be perfect, but even then, we can choose how to respond.

I dare you to own your choices and live an intentional life.

OWN HOW YOU CHOOSE TO RESPOND

Every human has four endowments: self-awareness, conscience, independent will and creative imagination. These give us the ultimate human freedom . . . The power to choose, to respond, to change.

—Stephen Covey

We can't control other people, but sometimes we think we can, or even should. But that's called manipulation, and it's wrong. The only thing we have the right to control is ourselves. That's not always easy. Taking ownership of our own responses and choices is a lot of work. Trying to do that on behalf of another or force it upon them is intrusive. What other people think and do is their decision. There's so much truth in that line. Pause and contemplate it. What we do have the right to own is our response to what others say and do. This is more powerful than I used to understand.

One of the symptoms of trauma is feeling helpless. There are things outside our control, but there's one thing we always do have the power to control, even if we're not aware of it. It's the power to respond, intentionally, using our choice. I call this our superpower.

When we tap into this superpower, it'll always work. I learned this from a man named Viktor E. Frankl. He suffered terribly in several of Germany's concentration camps during the Holocaust. He called this choice our last freedom. In his book *Man's Search For Meaning* he writes, *"Everything can be taken from a man but one thing: the last of human freedoms—to choose one's attitude in any given set of circumstances, to choose one's own way."*

I haven't suffered the loss of everything or been tortured. I can't relate to extinction ovens, dying of malnutrition in a third world country, or surviving natural disasters. But I do understand what he means by choice of response. We have our own unique circumstances to respond to, and what Victor Frankl discovered is *always available.*

It doesn't matter:

- If you're rich, poor, or in-between.
- If you live in the country, city, or slums.
- If you're male or female.
- If you're married, single, widowed, or divorced.
- If you're in jail, the hospital, or home free.

We have the God-given ability to choose how we respond to whatever comes our way. As children, we don't know this; but as adults, we can develop this. Choices have results. These results have a cause and effect (more on this later) which is why it's important to be intentional.

As adults, when we're treated improperly, we have the power to respond intentionally and speak up for ourselves. We don't have to put up with it.

But what if it's in the past? There's no going back in time. From personal experience, when delving into my childhood, I learned hidden things had gone wrong—things I had no control over. But as an adult, I have the power to respond positively or negatively. I chose the positive. I chose to forgive and understand and grow. Forgiveness is life-giving. If you choose negative, you'll get similar results.

By owning your response, you decide the direction your life will go.

OWN YOUR CHOICE TO RISE UP

We are more than the worst thing that's ever happened to us. All of us need to stop apologizing, for having been to hell and come back breathing.

—Clementine von Radics

Contrary to what many believe, our circumstances do *not* make us what we are. Yes, they impact our lives, but it doesn't end there. Circumstances reveal what's inside us. They don't have the power to control us—*we* are more powerful.

Do you question this with: *What about people in awful circumstances, or those who grow up with no opportunity, or those who have terrible things happen?*

Even in awful circumstances, the power of choice can lead you out and above those circumstances set on destroying you. Even when your circumstances suck, remember your superpower and look at these examples.

Tyler Perry[4] is a media mogul who suffered unimaginable childhood trauma. Not only was he violently abused by his father, but also molested by a male neighbor, a male nurse, a man at church, and a friend's mother. Physically, emotionally, verbally, and spiritually assaulted in his child soul, he used his imagination to escape, and as a teenager attempted suicide. Tyler calls his mother his saving grace because she gave him Jesus; and without faith in his life, he doesn't know where he'd be. In an interview with Oprah, Tyler thanked her for inspiring him to write. He started writing after seeing her on TV say, *"It's cathartic to start writing."* It helped him through his soul-searching. His therapeutic writings became the basis of his play *I Know I've Been Changed*, which became his first major success. Since then, he's produced so much more with his writings, including the creation of his most famous character, Madea. Tyler's overcoming has encouraged so many, empowering them to rise up too.

Bethany Hamilton[5] is known for her story in the movie *Soul Surfer*. She was born in Hawaii and began surfing when she was three to four years old. Trauma struck her life when at thirteen years old, she suffered a shark attack that almost killed her. A fourteen-foot Tiger Shark bit her left arm off, and she lost over half of the blood in her body. About three weeks later, she was up on her board surfing again. The following year her autobiography *Soul Surfer: A True Story of Faith, Family, and Fighting to Get Back on the Board* was published. She went on to win surfing championships and became a professional surfer. It's clear Bethany's ability to rise after tragedy came from her faith in God, the love of her family, and her positive attitude. She continues to touch and inspire others to overcome all over the world.

There are many other stories to be found where victims of childhood trauma have chosen to rise. It isn't about becoming rich and famous. It's about healing, growing, and living an intentional life. Everyone has something intent on destroying them. Choosing to blame others instead of tapping into the superpower inside, will rob you of your innate amazingness. If you're a follower of Jesus, He has promised you the power to overcome. *You can do all things through Christ. You are more than a conqueror. Greater is He that is in you.*

You can choose to rise up from tragedy and pain like the infamous Phoenix bird.

OWN YOUR STORY AND CHOOSE HOW IT ENDS

When we own our stories, we get to write a brave new ending.

—Brené Brown

Writing my first book taught me this. As I dealt with the pain from my childhood, I learned how much my perspective and choices would help or hinder my healing. What others had done and how I'd responded back in the day couldn't be changed. The effects left behind by trauma were involuntary, but they could be changed through healing—if I would take ownership of them. Those effects were my part of my story. Owning those parts of my story gave me the power to let go of what was outside of my control.

For example, when writing my first book, I had to let go of something that didn't belong to me. One of my primary childhood traumas occurred at church. The trauma was buried deep and affected every aspect of my life. Being healed of it was a long process. This letting go occurred early on before I understood the root of my trauma. When I found out the pastor responsible for my lifelong pain hung himself, I burst into tears because I blamed myself. Why would I blame myself? Two reasons. First, because the Spirit of Grace told me He held the pastor accountable, using a story in the Bible, and I didn't understand what He meant by accountable. Second, self-blame is what children do with trauma. Even though I was no longer a child, I still carried the self-blame. The Spirit of Grace comforted me. It wasn't my fault, and He helped me let go of the self-blame. What that pastor did was on him, not on me.

Owning my story is also how I gained the boldness to share. Fear of being wrong or judged tried to hold me back. But my story is my story, so what other people think of that is on them.

Your story is yours, no matter what others think. Your part is what you have control over. This is what gives you the power to write the ending.

Owning your part in *your* story empowers you to write a new ending.

OWN WHAT'S YOURS AND CHOOSE TO RESPECT BOUNDARIES

There is nothing noble in being superior to your fellow man; true nobility is being superior to your former self.

—Ernest Hemingway

The translation of the Polish proverb *Nie mój cyrk, nie moje malpy* is *not my circus, not my monkey* meaning *not my problem*. It's a great visual for drawing a boundary line between what belongs to you and what doesn't.

As you make changes in your life, you'll learn things. These things are for you to use in your life to heal, grow, and live—not impose into other people's lives.

For example, I learned a better way to raise children than how I was raised. Better than I raised my own kids. I learned it through a book by Danny Silk entitled *Loving Our Kids On Purpose*. Imagine I go to a grocery store or park, and see a child acting out. The child is screaming at their parent or thrashing on the ground, having a tantrum. It's not my business to speak to the child or the adult with my opinion on the matter. It doesn't matter if I mean well, and I need to keep my *"wisdom"* to myself. Grocery stores and parks are public places where people have no authority over others. A momentary knowledge of any situation doesn't factor in the humans involved, or how the situation came to be. Intruding is an invasion of their boundaries. Unless someone is committing a crime, mind your own business.

I remember reading a story about a man on a subway with his children. It was late, and the kids were loud and rambunctious. A stranger complained to the dad about the children's behavior and how the dad ought to be controlling them. The stranger was met with a response he hadn't expected. The dad apologetically explained how they'd been at the hospital all day, where his wife—the children's mom—had died. The stranger felt bad for saying anything, meddling where he had no business.

Owning what belongs to you prevents you from being critical of others.

OWN THE CHOICES THAT WILL BENEFIT YOU

When the challenges are yours the victories are sweet.

—Danielle Bernock

Healing from my childhood trauma took a long time. Years. There were plenty of choices I had to make along the way. You'll have various choices to make as well. Some are easier than others, but all of them are important.

One choice is the decision to become well, to become whole. It takes a fight to become well and whole. This decision to fight for your wellbeing takes courage, which is why I have an entire chapter for you on this. You can do this—*because you matter*, and I'll prove it to you.

Another choice I made was to enter counseling. I'm a big advocate of this. There's no shame in seeking professional help. Counseling is for the brave, not the weak. I'm also of the belief that you need the right counselor. I had one early in my healing journey that was both helpful and harmful. You want helpful. Later, when I was writing my first book, I started looking for a counselor again. I believed it was a wise choice. I went through a few before I found a good fit. I almost gave up, but I'm glad I didn't. It was a wiser choice than I imagined. I had much more healing to go through than I'd been aware of.

I stayed with my counselor this time for five and a half years. When and how my counselor said that I was ready to stop surprised me. She said I was handling life well, and if there was a textbook success story for counseling, I was it. I was stunned, especially because I didn't feel ready that day. I continued with her counsel for a few more months before I felt I was handling my life like she said I was.

At my last session with her, I brought up what she said, about being a success story, and asked her what made me successful. Without hesitation, she said, "Courage." She reminded me of when our time together first began. I was terrified of everything: my feelings, my thoughts, my situation, my past, how to deal with things, etc. But I'd taken courage and confronted everything, and put into practice what she instructed, learned the skills, and am using them. She said I was ready, and she was proud of me. I could've cried.

I surveyed several counselors and pastors for their professional opinion on the matter. I asked them what people needed to be successful in healing, and what would hinder them. The overwhelming response to what helps a person succeed was willingness.

- Willingness to take ownership of what belongs to them.
- Willingness to accept and admit they need help.
- Willingness to feel and confront their issues.
- Willingness to change their perceptions.
- Willingness to make the changes necessary along the way.
- Willingness is a choice.

Another thing they said helps a person successfully to heal is support. It's important for them to know they're not alone and they're loved. Although this book can't be your life's personal support system—it's a book, not a person—the information in here is designed to support you, providing tools you need. It's in choosing to take ownership of these tools you'll own everything else you need.

Take ownership of your choices one by one to arrive at your healing.

KEY POINTS

- Taking ownership of one's life involves choices.
- We can't change what's happened, but we have the power to choose how to proceed.
- By owning your response, you get to decide the direction your life will go now.
- Even in awful circumstances, the power of choice can lead you out and above those circumstances set on destroying you.
- Owning your part in your story empowers you to write a new ending.
- Owning what belongs to you prevents you from being critical of others.
- Willingness is a choice.

YOU CAN ASK GOD FOR HELP

Dear God, help me to be willing. Help me make the choices I need to, the ones that are good for me. Help me choose to rise above the things that have tried to destroy me.

NOTES

How Jackie Took Ownership of Her Life

When you make a decision, you change your life.

—Jackie Trottmann

Jackie and I met at the 2018 Tribe Writers' Conference in Franklin, Tennessee. We spent time together at one of the meetups and became friends. She has a wonderfully positive outlook on life and a beautiful smile. While interviewing Jackie for this book, she shared three noticeable times where she took ownership of her life. I found that quite compelling.

Once, is commendable, three times, is remarkable. Each time she did, she had the same impetus driving her choices. One was a deep resolve *"to not be dependent on anyone."* This resolve drove her through mid-life. The other was to live life with joy and flow, a lifestyle she writes about and teaches.

Jackie explained to me what she meant by "flow." *"The first part of flow is to fancy something."* When she decided to go back to school for a business degree in 1977, she fancied art, music, and business. This is what led her to obtain a job in advertising.

That single choice launched a 30-year career in that industry.

It was the first of the three she shared with me.

She enjoyed working in the advertising industry at first. However, deep below the surface rumbled the pain of her childhood soul wounds. Their eruption would lead to the second big pivot point in her life. But first, we'll look at the trauma that caused her soul wounds.

As I listened to Jackie share her story, I could hear the sadness in her voice. She told me about a sudden change in her dad when she was seven or eight-years-old. She reminisced about their time together. How he'd take her places and how she felt his love using the words *"the apple of his eye."* But then his once warm demeanor turned cold, and she felt abandoned.

Imagine what that felt like!

But as she went on with her story, the cause of her rumbling soul wounds became clear in addition to how they'd been buried so long.

Jackie's dad was an alcoholic and later diagnosed as bi-polar. Violent outbursts ensued. Jackie described her mom as a true British Brit with a stiff upper lip. Because of how her parents were choosing to cope with life, the frequent outbursts were never discussed. She lived on high alert all the time just like the family dog who would run and hide under the stereo when her father's car pulled in the driveway. But Jackie had no bedroom to run and hide in, so she hid inside herself.

The house had two bedrooms. Her older brother got one of the bedrooms, and her parents had the other, leaving Jackie to sleep in the living room. A living room offers no privacy for a little girl growing up. Jackie loved to draw and dreamed of being an artist. She kept all her artwork on the coffee table because there was no other place for it.

One day when she came home from school, the coffee table was empty. She asked her dad where her artwork was. He barked that her papers made a mess and he threw them in the trash. She ran to retrieve them, but they'd been taken away by the garbage truck. Devastated, she stuffed her feelings just like her mom taught her whenever she cried. Her mom would say, *"now, now, don't cry—get it together."*

Jackie stuffed her feelings down so deeply she forgot about them until much later in life. Yet those feelings didn't forget her.

In this book, I take great pains to make the point—if you don't deal with your feelings, they will deal with you.

For example, instead of following her dream to be an artist when Jackie made plans for college, she dismissed her talent telling herself she wasn't Norman Rockwell. She pursued voice instead, telling herself it was a better choice until she dismissed her singing talent. She told herself she wasn't going to be Barbara Streisand and went home to do something more practical. But that didn't go according to her plan.

Her plan of practical turned into misery. That's when her resolve led to that first decision I mentioned—to go back to school.

But when she made that decision, she didn't understand it was the unaddressed trauma from her childhood that was keeping her from becoming her true self. She was still efficient at stuffing whatever pains were in her soul—until they would not be denied.

Enter her second big life change decision.

After thirty years in the advertising industry and getting married, she was miserable and didn't understand why.

In 2001, a friend told her about a book on codependency. Standing in the bookstore flipping through the pages Jackie gasped.

"This is me!"

She always thought her dad's alcoholism was his problem. But now it was hers. Although she wasn't addicted to alcohol, she was a food addict and workaholic who didn't know who she was. She realized she was doing all the "shoulds" in her life, what everyone else wanted her to do or expected her to do.

How Jackie put this epiphany was *"I've been doing my whole life what I **should** be doing, and I'm not doing anything that I **want** to do."*

She had none of the joy she writes about now.

Healing from the trauma of her childhood that caused her codependency and discovering who she was came at a cost. Completely broken Jackie left her job, husband, dream home, and security in 2002. How Jackie put it was, *"I didn't know what I was going to do, but I knew I had to get out, or my soul was going to die."*

Jackie was scared and alone like the little girl without a bedroom again. As she got down to the last nickel in her checking account, her deep resolve rose up within her to take ownership of the situation. Calling friends for job leads and using an offer to leverage a better job she landed a position as Vice President of Marketing. Nine months later she met Robert (who became her husband).

Due to her decision, Jackie's life took on a new trajectory. Through taking up yoga and learning to listen to her body, she stopped using food to cope. Leaning into her faith, Jackie worked hard to deal with her childhood trauma. She started learning how to be still, let go, and how to trust. Trust herself and trust others. As she let go of the emotional weight, her physical weight dropped off with it.

In 2016 Jackie took her third bold move of ownership.

She let all her marketing clients go to focus on her writing again. She started the journey to write eight years earlier. But this new direction had its difficulties. She found more parts of her that needed growth, namely how she valued herself.

When Jackie left her high paying job, and fancy title to be self-employed in 2008, her sense of value fell under attack. She journaled her feelings finding the root trauma in that little girl who had her artwork thrown in the trash. The buried emotions had been saying *your work is trash.*

She knows better now. In fact, when sharing her story about not being Norman Rockwell, she chuckled, "*Now I can go back to my 18-year-old self and say, of course, you're not Norman Rockwell—you're you!*"

Becoming her true self empowered her. The online author marketing skills she was learning brought her opportunity when her husband was laid off in 2009. With them, she built a web development company that provided for the family for seven years until she was able to let those clients go to once again focus fully on her writing.

Throughout her journey, Jackie's tenacious nature served her. She climbed over numerous mountains of pain to find her joy and flow. Now she's a full-time writer, speaker, and mentor who has published two books and three guided meditations.

Why did Jackie make the decision to be a writer?

"*Writing, creating, and mentoring feeds my soul. I'm in my joy there, and that's where I want to live. I write about joy and flow, and it's taken me all this time in my life to get to that place.*"

Find out more about Jackie and what she has to offer in the endnotes.

CHAPTER 4

Owning Your Value

To be deeply loved, means a willingness to cut yourself wide open, exposing your vulnerabilities . . . hopes, hurts, fears and flaws. Hiding behind the highlight reel of who you are, is the real you and that person is just as worthy of love. There is nothing more terrifying or fulfilling, than complete love, it's worth the risk . . . reach for it.

—Jaeda DeWalt

HOW TO BEGIN

When you've struggled with your value and worth, the idea of *owning* it is difficult. Owning your value when you see little or none begins by considering the possibility. Imagine not struggling with self-esteem. Taking ownership of your life involves seeing and owning your value.

I dare you to own your value and your worthiness of love.

OWN YOU'RE LOVED BEYOND REASON

The LORD appeared to us in the past, saying: I have loved you with an everlasting love; I have drawn you with unfailing kindness.

—Jeremiah

Everyone knows loving and being loved is the greatest need of humanity. Science has proven this. Lack of love is responsible for all the pain in the world. Being loved isn't enough. Loving others isn't enough. We need both. Love lives in a circle. It's perpetual. When we feel unloved, we treat people unlovingly. This behavior disseminates a lack of love.

The only way to break out of the negative circle of feeling unloved is to own being loved. If that's too hard, own the possibility of being loved. Think to yourself *just maybe*. Consider it. Roll it around in your head. Just maybe.

Owning the possibility is the beginning. But for the circle of love to be strong in your heart, and subsequently, in your life, it needs a secure origin. Where does this love come from? It must start somewhere. I believe it originates with God because God is love. Our humanity wants to know where God came from. The Bible says He always was. He was before we were. Humans have a beginning. We're born, and we die. This love has no beginning and no end. It's eternal. Eternal love is difficult to grasp.

The God I've come to know loves us more than we can fathom in our finite humanity. The Bible says He loves us with an *everlasting love*. What's everlasting love? Humanity doesn't display it to one another, so it's hard for us to imagine. It takes daring to believe, or faith. We need this all-encompassing love. We crave it because we were created for love. We tap into and enjoy it when we own the possibility of its truth. That possibility is like a tiny seed. Take it and plant it in your heart, and the God who loves you with an everlasting love will cause that seed to grow. I've done this, and it's life-changing. I didn't understand it when I dared to own the possibility. I still don't completely. But I enjoy it. I don't expect to fully grasp it until I'm in His presence. While alive in this world, my mind will question. My mind is limited to the natural except for the places where God has given me insight. This illumination of truth in my understanding is that seed growing. It's a spiritual work and a gift from the one who loves beyond reason in an everlasting way. Allowing this love to cycle through me is living in a circle of love.

Own the possibility and begin to know love like you never have before.

OWN YOU'RE WORTHY OF CELEBRATION

The Lord your God is with you. He is a hero who saves you. He happily rejoices over you, renews you with his love, and celebrates over you with shouts of joy.

—Zephaniah

God celebrates you. Those words are hard to believe for many. What's your response when you read them? Read them again— God celebrates you. You. As is. Where you are. Flaws and all. Do you believe it? I didn't for the longest time. It took me thirty-four years to believe it, to be fully convinced. That's a long time. Some might say too long. *Why did it take so long? Will it take me that long?* I can't say how long it'll take you. There were multiple things in my way. One was the trauma that happened to me at church as a child. I had numerous wounds in my soul. Multiple lies I had been convinced were true. But truth wins over lies. Now I believe God celebrates you and me!

Believe you're worthy of being celebrated. I believe your worth is established by God. Not as a result of anything you did or do. It has nothing to do with talent, personality, where you're born, what race or nationality you are. It's all about the heart of our creator. He delights in us. He has put enormous value on us and deemed us worthy of life and love. Worthy of redemption through the precious blood of Jesus who laid down His life of His own free will because we matter—because you matter. The Bible illustrates God's celebration of us through dancing over us with joy, the shepherd rejoicing carrying the lamb, and the father of the prodigal throwing a party.

Dare to see your value and own God's celebration of you.

OWN YOUR BELOVEDNESS LIKE JESUS DID

Many times in the Old Testament, God refers to human beings as His beloved. But when God called Jesus His beloved, Jesus did something truly remarkable: He believed Him. And He lived every moment of His life fully convinced of His identity.

—Jonathan Martin

To be beloved of God is to be cherished, precious, loved deeply, and unconditionally. My life completely changed when I owned this belovedness. Knowing I'm loved by God deeply and unconditionally provided an unshakeable sense of security. The knowing I'm talking about is deeper than *I know that*. We can understand English and say we accept something is true without truly *knowing*. It can be superficial. We just agree with our minds. But to truly *know*, there's deep intimacy the Spirit of Grace offers.

Our world is full of relationship danger and betrayal. Grasping this safe union feels fake, elusive, and too good to be true. Religion hasn't helped—but that's in another chapter. I struggled to know this belovedness. It felt imaginary and intangible. Until the day I became fully convinced, and I owned it. This inspired me to write a little book called *Love's Manifesto*[6] to help others feel seen, known, and loved. This love is a forever love.

The Bible says God the Father loves us as much as He loves Jesus. He called Jesus His Beloved Son before any miracles were performed or one sermon was preached. In fact, in addition to calling Jesus Beloved, God said He was well pleased with Him. Jesus knew the pleasure of being beloved apart from anything He did. This empowered Him to endure the temptations in the wilderness that followed. During that time of temptation, the devil addressed Jesus as the son of God but left off the word beloved.

Knowing I'm beloved of God changed everything. I know my value and worth. It makes me strong on the inside.

Owning this state of being beloved has the potential to change your life and all your relationships. Seeing yourself as truly beloved affects your behavior and how you treat others. The grace is unending. You're worthy of this belovedness because God says so. It's not because of anything you say or do. It all rests securely on Him. He did this on purpose, knowing our imperfection and our ability to screw it up somehow. We can rest in His love.

You can own your belovedness in the sight of God and sense His pleasure.

OWN YOUR INHERENT VALUE

So God created mankind in his own image, in the image of God he created them; male and female he created them.

—Moses

Where do you get your value from? Your answer will define your struggle, as well as your remedy. If you attach your value to success or people's opinions, it will fluctuate. If you attach it to something unchanging, you can have security.

The world will put requirements on you to qualify your value. It'll be performance-based, or something outside your control.

Where you were born, the color of your skin, your gender, for example. The value God ascribes to you is unchanging. God considers you valuable right now—*as is*—because you were created in His image. You're the object of His affection. The Bible says Jesus came and gave His lifeblood to demonstrate this amazing love. I believe this. God did this because He puts enormous value on us. It's called inherent, fundamental, innate, intrinsic, inborn. Because of your inherent God-given value, you're always loved, celebrated, and called beloved.

Because of your value, you have amazing potential. Failing to own your value keeps you from achieving your potential and enjoying your life.

Owning your inherent value is foundational to taking ownership of your life.

OWN YOUR "*SELF*" BECAUSE YOU MATTER

For God so loved the world that he gave his one and only Son, that whoever believes in him shall not perish but have eternal life.

—John

Who you are, belongs to you. Fully owning your *self* (or failing to) will determine your life. *Self* is not a bad word, and your *self* is not something God wants to destroy. If you're a believer in Jesus Christ and that sounds strange, please hear me out. Christians aren't called to be void of *self* because your *self* is your soul. The Bible says to *possess* our souls using patience. To possess our soul, we need to take ownership of our *self*. It's the *self* that makes the decision to become a follower of Jesus, or not, in the first place. If you decide to, it doesn't mean you're supposed to eliminate your *self*. If you did, you'd no longer exist. Instead, the goal is to train *self* with the truth.

I struggled for years with my value, thinking I had no right to exist due to the multiple childhood traumas I'd suffered. This was exacerbated by misunderstanding the doctrine of dying to *self* that I was taught in church. I thought it meant I wasn't supposed to exist anymore, and it confused me. I discovered I'm not alone in that struggle. That feeling of being alone was another part of my struggle. Learning my value—that I matter—*little ol' me*, was epic. The Spirit of Grace showed me Jesus died to be joined to me—*not* exterminate me.

Contrary to how some portray Him, God is not some alien being on a quest to assimilate His creation. That's not love, and God is Love. Love seeks union. God desires union with you because He loves you. Because you matter. To enjoy union with God, you need to own your *self*. You can't give what isn't yours. Through union, we're not lost; but, we gain a oneness, a partnership. We become *we* instead of separate and alone.

You're an amazing creation of God. You matter. I believe when we join ourselves to Jesus, it's plugging into the power source of life. It's like a lamp, a toaster, or other electrical appliance plugged into a wall socket so it can do what it's designed for. Jesus provides life and power. With Him, we can do what we're designed to do. The power is in the connection.

Owning your *self* is how to live with intention.

OWN YOUR UNIQUENESS: WE'RE ALL DIFFERENT

"Rest in your God-breathed worth. Stop holding your breath, hiding your gifts, ducking your head, dulling your roar, distracting your soul, stilling your hands, quieting your voice, and satiating your hunger with the lesser things of this world."

—Sarah Bessey

The world is a big place. We want to make a difference in it, but we face obstacles. One is comparison. We measure and judge how we think we're doing by others. We all do it. But it's a problem. Comparing ourselves with others is unfair. Measuring your value, your success, and identity to someone else's appearance of greatness is a problem. Why? Because it cripples self-esteem, making you powerless. It creates an obstacle between you and your hopes, dreams, and purposes. When you compare yourself to someone else, you judge in favor of them or you. There's a winner and a loser. Every. Time.

You're only better compared to some, but worse to others. Comparing creates jealousy, competition, pecking orders, and rivalries. No one thrives in this environment. Comparison is based on incomplete information. You don't fully know the person you're comparing yourself to. Unless it's your bestie you probably only know the edited version of the person's life; or, maybe it's one thing they did you're judging yourself by. It's information out of context and false perception. Comparison sees only differences where there's no win/win. Comparing yourself to someone else is apples to oranges, pineapples to watermelons. No one is the same, and that's not a bad thing.

When my kids were small, we had a book *Bible Time Nursery Rhymes* by Emily Hunter. A favorite was *I Am Me and You Are You*. It cited and celebrated how we're all different. It listed everyday things we all do but how we do them differently: standing, walking, smiling, singing, writing, drawing, sleeping, and more. The reason she gave stuck with my kids, and with me: *God made one of me—not two*! I had no problem seeing the value in my children's uniqueness. I struggled to see it in myself until I did the following:

Make a careful exploration of who you are and the work you have been given, and then sink yourself into that. Don't be impressed with yourself. Don't compare yourself with others. Each of you must take responsibility for doing the creative best you can with your own life. (emphasis mine)

Finding value in your true unique self and owning it sets you free from the need to compare. You matter—as is. It took most of my life to learn my value. That I mattered—as is. The biggest change came through the endeavor of writing that first book. I made a *careful exploration of who I was* and emerged with an entirely new mindset of who I am. After writing and publishing the book, my life became as different as the caterpillar is from the butterfly; however, just as the butterfly carries some of the parts of the caterpillar, I discovered old things in me—things like comparison. A quote from the movie *The Princess Bride* helped me. The villain (Vizzini) snorts a question to Princess Buttercup.

I suppose you think you're brave, don't you?

Only compared to some.

Her wisdom and humility arrested me.

There will always be those who appear better, or worse, but the truth is they're only different. Different isn't bad all by itself. Our behavior and choices can be good or bad; but, our inherent value is incomparable. Being different than others doesn't make you less valuable than them, or them more important than you. It doesn't mean you're doing something wrong, or that they are. ***Be sure to do what you should, for then you will enjoy the personal***

satisfaction of having done your work well, *and you won't need to compare yourself to anyone else.* (Emphasis mine)

I dare you to take ownership of your uniqueness and remind yourself of *your* value and *your own* purpose or path. Why? Because you matter and your unique path and purpose matter too. You're not an accident. God made you on purpose. He put things in you that are only in you. He desires for you to fulfill the callings placed within you. We do this by owning our uniqueness because comparing ourselves with other people is the wrong measure. Instead, measure your progress on your *own* life journey. The rhyme is true: *I am me, and you are you.* Comparison is poisonous.

You're unique with enormous value: your life, your thoughts, your feelings, your actions, your choices, your dreams, your everything. You're an irreplaceable individual with your own strengths and weakness. And here's where your power is: it's your choice. It's up to you what you do with it. Will you own it?

Even though we know we're all different, we try to be like everyone else. Our need for belonging drives us. We feel our differences separate us. They do but in a good way. Each of us is unique. We may share various characteristics with others, but no two of us are exactly the same. Even identical twins have differences. It's in owning our uniqueness that we can be our true selves. It takes courage. Some find it easier than others. For some, their personality gives them boldness. Others may have been raised to be confident and bold. That second one is evidence when we lack confidence. We can gain it. We can learn. We can train ourselves. It may take a lot of work, but because we matter, it's worth it.

Imagine a field of wildflowers—hundreds in variation. It's beautiful. Now imagine all those flowers are the same. It's quite a different picture. For your true beauty to be revealed, you need to embrace who you are—quirks and all. Strengths and weaknesses. I dare you. Dare to believe the world needs you and own your uniqueness.

Here is a poem I started reading out loud to myself to remind me to be who I am. If you like it, you can do the same.

DARE TO BELIEVE

You can't be all things to all people
You can't do all things at once
You can't do all things equally well
You can't do all things better than everyone else
Your humanity is showing just like everyone else's

So:
Find out who you are, and be that
Decide what comes first, and do that
Discover your strengths, and use them
Learn not to compete with others
Because no one else is in the contest of *being you*

Dare to accept your own uniqueness
Dare to set priorities and make decisions
Dare to accept your limitations
Dare to give yourself the respect that is due
Dare to speak up

Dare to Believe:
That you are a wonderful, unique person
That you are a once-in-all-history event
Embrace the privilege to be who you are – Be!
Life is not a problem to solve, but a gift to cherish
Embrace and enjoy life!

KEY POINTS

- Taking ownership of your life involves seeing and owning your value.
- When we feel unloved, we treat people unlovingly.
- God celebrates you. You. As is. Where you are. Flaws and all. Do you believe it?
- To be beloved of God is to be cherished, precious, loved deeply, and unconditionally.
- Where you get your value from will define your struggle, as well as your remedy.
- Owning your *self* is how to live with intention.
- Your uniqueness is poisoned by comparison.

YOU CAN ASK GOD FOR HELP

Thank you, God, for loving and valuing me so much you sent Jesus. Thank you, Jesus, for loving and valuing me so much you came and did everything necessary to reconnect us. Help me see the value you put in me and train my *self* in your truth.

NOTES

How John Took Ownership of His Life

You need to make sure that you do good self-care, and that you monitor yourself. Because if you don't, you will self-eliminate.

—John Thurman

John is a man of undeniable inner strength. Like tungsten, but with a blend of joy and compassion making him approachable. I walked up to John and introduced myself at my first Tribe Conference. It was his first, also and we became friends. I quickly learned the plethora of ways John works to serve others. I had no idea he had been through PTSD himself until I interviewed him.

John spent his childhood in a solid middle-class home. He said growing up in a small town *"you couldn't get away with anything,"* and we chuckled together. His family was service-oriented, and he dreamed of helping others when he grew up. *"It seems like I've always been involved in helping other people. The journey through my education and life experiences. It just continued to constantly affirm and reaffirm that."* As I listened to John tell me story after story, I saw how helping others is in his DNA. But his service cost him.

As a teenager, John took ownership of what kind of person he wanted to be. While attending North Carolina Outward Bound school, he chose to internalize their motto. "To serve. To strive. And, not to yield." He was sixteen years old. John told me the school's philosophy was *"to push you further than you thought you could go and then push you some more."* This was to develop inner strength so the students could endure hard things. John confessed he didn't appreciate this training for years, but it clearly built intestinal fortitude and resilience within him. Now he passes the lesson along to others, *"there's more in you than you know."*

John went to a Christian liberal arts college, got married, attended Southwestern Theological Seminary, and joined the Army reserves. When not on assignment he ministered to youth and singles, was an associate pastor, and did some work with Emergency Medical Services.

In 1986 tragedy struck. *"I was getting ready to move out to New Mexico. My brother was in a car wreck, and he was burned to death."* It was horrible, but John was able to work through his grief because of his training and experience. Being around death was part of being in the military and ministry. John went into service mode for his family. *"I kinda went on autopilot."* Many other friends came and ministered to John's family also. Three weeks later, he and his wife completed their move to New Mexico fifteen hundred miles away from family.

They were in New Mexico for three weeks when John was sent to Fort Huachuca on special assignment. Six weeks after the loss of his brother, he took ownership of his own trauma using his training. *"Don't isolate. Find people you can trust and bare your soul. Listen to what they say."* He spoke with George Smith, who was an LDS Army Chaplain and grief counselor. Baring his soul, John was met with wisdom. George asked how many deaths he deals within a year, and John told him, *"You're fine. What's going to happen is in six months or so (once you get settled in) is you'll probably wake up at two and three in the morning and have a really deep crying time."* It happened just as George predicted. A deep cleansing quiet grieving took place in John's soul. *"This side of heaven, I knew I would never see him again and kind of worked through that."* After six months, he felt he could move on.

Another change was about to take place altering John's career path. He got a job at a church. *"I was an associate pastor with sin-*

gle adults and young people counseling." John already understood that working in ministry isn't always as *"pure and clean as you thought it was,"* but this job dealt him a form of betrayal. In less than a year, the pastor he worked with left the church. This caused the rest of the staff to be put on severance. Unexpectedly employed John thought about his future. He had the degree and certifications for counseling but lacked being licensed. A few courses later, John remedied that.

"And it was shortly after that Desert Storm came along and I got mobilized."

And so, it began: the silent building of John's PTSD. John had done a lot of work in mental health, crisis, and being a chaplain. Due to his experience, he got a call to work in the burn unit. *"And I was like, oh, man, do I want to go there?"* He called and spoke with a friend of like faith and shared his reservation for the assignment. *"My brother burned five years ago. The last place I thought the Army would stick me is in a burn unit."* His friend told him it was his call but thought John's faith in Christ would be enough. John took the challenge and went.

The chaplain at the burn unit offered to transfer John, and he declined. John felt sent, but at the same time, knew he needed a safety net. He asked the team to back him up and be there for him, and they were. There was one guy he got close to named Irv. It was Irv that debriefed John every day. The first week was the hardest. For seven months, he faced the intensity. When John got home, he wasn't sleeping, but he *"just dealt with it."* He wasn't having *"any thoughts or any type of intrusive things,"* so he sucked it up.

A year later, John was in another burn unit. This time it was a civilian who went to his church. There was a tragic accident. John's pastor called asking him to go see the young man involved. *"He's been electrocuted. He's burned. His arm burned off just below the elbow."* John questioned his ability to deal with the situation. When deployed, he had a team he worked with. Here he'd be alone. When John got to the parking lot, he had a panic attack. He sat there *"praying the Lord's prayer and recited the 23rd psalm four times just so I could kind of get centered."* After gathering himself, he went to the burn unit.

John described the smell as the first thing to assault him. The stench was a combination of burnt tissue and the thick Silvadene cream they put on the burns. Focusing on his breathing, John was met by the nurse. They talked about what to expect and John's experience. But John knew better than to rely on his experience alone. He asked her if they could talk after *"because an hour ago, I hadn't planned to be sitting with a guy who's been burned."* She agreed. He went in to see the young man. John prayed as he entered the room, seeing the bandaged arm and his newlywed wife. He met with the nurse after to debrief. For several months John continued to minister to the young man and his family helping them process through their trauma. Little did John know this would come back to bite him.

A year later, the triggers began. A friend of his had been exposed to a few burn victims while working as a chaplain with First Responders. He talked with John about it, describing his experience. Cascading memories and intrusive thoughts started bothering John. He responded with his training talking himself through it, acknowledging a trigger had been tripped. This was just the beginning of his PTSD.

Another incident occurred intensifying the trauma within John. He was driving his son home from a sleepover, and John saw his doctor's nurse giving CPR to a guy on the sidewalk. *"There were ten to twelve people standing around not helping so I got out of the car, my son got out with me."* John and the woman worked on the man with CPR and breathing for him for about fifteen minutes before the ambulance arrived. But he died. They weren't able to save him. This was deeply troubling for John. *"I went and talked to a physician, and a couple friends to debrief on that. The combination of being involved with that burn. And that friend talking about the scene he was on, and then this unsuccessful resuscitation. That's when it blossomed."*

John was working at a Christian counseling agency. Two of his colleagues dealt with trauma and a therapy called EMDR. He asked them to help him. *"I spent a lot of time talking with them and doing some really hard work and being able to kind of recalibrate that. See it for what it was. Because part of what my life has been about has been helping people."* John is what is known as a sheepdog. It's a term in law enforcement and the military. They're the ones who run toward trouble when they see it to bring about a better outcome. But running toward trouble exposes a sheepdog to stuff that can hurt them. John found himself wounded.

As John relayed this story to me, he quoted Friedrich W. Nietzsche and then elaborated on it.

"Beware that, when fighting monsters, you yourself do not become a monster . . . for when you gaze long into the abyss. The abyss gazes also into you."

What that means to John is: *"When you work with fire and EMS. When you work with people, who are troubled. You are staring into the dark abyss of human suffering. If you are not vigilant, take care of yourself, you'll self-eliminate."* Human suffering is the abyss, and that abyss stares back. That abyss will bite you if you don't pay attention. *"If you don't take the care of yourself, mentally, physically, spiritually, and emotionally, you will self-eliminate. You will render yourself useless. I want to be in the fight for the long haul because I love what I do."*

John was diligent to check in with his friends and colleagues for a couple of years. He took ownership of his recovery using journaling, talk therapy, and a technique called tapping. He briefly explained tapping to me but directed me to do more research. Tapping does bilateral stimulation in the brain like EMDR, but you do it yourself. John is thankful he knew what was happening and didn't get lost in the PTSD. He was armed with the knowledge of his training and surrounded by "*a group of friends that love the Lord. They would pray for me, but also help me therapeutically and give me tools.*"

John's hard work to recover from PTSD was validated by the VA. After being evaluated by a psychologist for PTSD, he was told, "*You're a good therapist. I can't diagnose you with PTSD, because you treated yourself well. But you have a little disability that relates to your sleep. This relates to the trauma.*" John is grateful for the validation. Yes, he did have PTSD, he's dealt with it, and the VA believes him. John credits his recovery to the good team of people who surrounded him and his tenacity to fight for it. John's sleep issues are much better these days.

Healing from trauma is a choice. John tells his clients they have a say in how they move forward. He never says it's easy. In fact, one of his clients reported to him a few years after her recovery. "*I believed in you. I believed you when you told me it was up to me, and I had the power to do what I needed to do if I wanted God's help. That day when you asked me what I wanted, I felt scared spitless and empowered.*" She chose to turn her pain into power and became a new stronger person.

John has been in the people-helping business for over forty years. He believes healthy relationships, that are honest and real are key to emotional and mental health. Therapy has its place. It's what John does for a living, so he doesn't diminish it. But if the choice to recover isn't made, a person remains a victim. In Manhattan, New York, ten years after the Twin Towers terrorist attack research "*found that most people experienced post-traumatic growth. They had friends, neighbors, relatives, colleagues, church, and they had faith. And very few of them needed therapy. When post-traumatic growth really kicks in. We see them able to be not just a survivor, but a thriver and overcomer."*

Find out more about John and what he has to offer in the endnotes.

CHAPTER 5

Owning Your Courage

To be loved and to love, takes courage. To be fully seen is incredibly rare and breathtaking. We lower our masks and see a celestial inner being. It is our full self—the supernova as well as the black holes. Our fears and doubts. Our anger and joy . . . This is love.

—Carolyn Riker

HOW TO BEGIN

Courage is a powerful tool. Utilizing yours will make the difference between success and failure in owning your life. I want you to succeed. I believe in you. There's courage inside you. Courage is strength in the face of opposition—for example, pain, grief, danger, discouragement, failure, and fear. Whenever we want to do something new, fear always shows up. Courage sees, feels, and recognizes the fear or obstacle. It then digs in its heels pushing forward to accomplish your goal.

I dare you to use your courage and become brave.

OWN LOVE'S POWER OVER FEAR

There is no fear in love; but perfect love casts out fear: because fear involves torment.

—John

Fear is something we all deal with—some more than others. I used to be plagued by fear. Not the natural kind like heights or normal nervousness, but a fear that was spiritual in nature. The idea of being free of fear was a mirage. Even so, I pursued freedom like a parched desert traveler chases an oasis hallucination brought on by dehydration. Fear tormented me, and I was desperate to be free. I gained measures of freedom but still felt bound.

Then something happened. I had an encounter showing me freedom was available. Hope bloomed in my heart. It took place at a small weekend conference hosted by a ministry we were partners with. At this weekend, we not only heard great teaching, but we also had one on one contact with the leaders of the ministry. We had conversations, asked questions, and were given resources. Through personal encounters, I saw how I could be free of that spirit of fear because they were. They said the spirit of fear wasn't trying to scare us. Its goal was to intimidate us into letting go of our trust in what God had said to us. That was a completely different way for me to look at it. Through this new perspective, I saw how fear was undermining the love of God for me. What a game-changer.

I was familiar with the verse in the Bible, *"perfect love drives out fear,"* but misunderstood how. I worked at loving God and developing the characteristics of love. I used the familiar list beginning with *"love is patient, love is kind . . ."* but it wasn't working for me.

Perhaps you've done what I did. Worked at it and failed. How I win against fear is knowing and trusting the love of God for me.

Not superficial. Not conditional. Beloved, like we talked about in the previous chapter. Right here. Right now. As is. All of it depends on His love. Not mine. He loved me first. By accepting His love apart from anything I do, it produces courage when I face fear. I sense I'm not alone, and God is on my side.

The second half of the verse above is *"He that feareth is not made perfect in love."* I used to read that as something I had to perform and beat myself up when I failed. I was wrong. Those words are a mirror to see how far I am on my journey overcoming fear. It's His love that does the work, not me.

Spiritual fear loses power when we know and believe God's love for us.

OWN THE NEWNESS: NEW THINKING CREATES NEW LIFE

Be made new in your hearts and in your thinking. Be that new person who was made to be like God, truly good and pleasing to him.

—Paul

When we get new things like clothes, cars, and toys, it's exciting and fun. But when it comes to new thinking, we can feel intimidated, scared, and confused.

- Intimidated because we understand it won't be easy to change how we think. It's a lot of work and takes mental, emotional, and spiritual energy. We question if we can succeed.
- Scared because we're familiar with how we think now. Familiarity carries an element of comfort, but new thinking is unknown and feels foreign. Unknown things carry an element of fear to hold us back.

- Confused because we understand the need to think differently but don't know how or where to begin.

We may question the truth or validity of new information. For example, once I came across a television minister preaching the grace of God in a manner I'd not heard before. What he said sounded too good to be true. I was scared to be misled. Some people say he preaches a false doctrine. It intimidated me. But instead of backing away, I investigated. I took the new information to God through prayer and study. I was like the Berean's in the Bible *"who received the word with all readiness of mind, and searched the scriptures daily, whether those things were so."* I prayed for wisdom and direction. I'm glad I was courageous with the scary newness. It's been foundational to building the new thinking patterns that have changed my life. Owning the newness empowered me to press through the difficulties of intimidation, fear, and confusion.

New thinking patterns produce new behavior. By repeating the new actions, the newness gives way to familiarity becoming a habit. This is the way to create a new life for yourself. Research and prayer are good tools to use in building new thinking.

A new life awaits you through courageous new thinking.

OWN YOUR HEALING: CHILDHOOD TRAUMA CAN BE HEALED

I've experienced several different healing methodologies over the years—counseling, self-help seminars, and I've read a lot—but none of them will work unless you really want to heal.

—Lindsay Wagner

As I said earlier, there are various things that can traumatize a child. Children cope with trauma differently than adults. They can be suffering trauma and not realize it due to psychological immaturity. Everything is learning. Some children are fortunate to get help during or following trauma. This is usually the case when it's obvious an event occurred causing trauma—for example, physical or sexual abuse.

But there's also emotional, verbal and spiritual abuse which oftentimes go undetected. When that happens, the adult carries the side effects of the pain which manifest in various ways: flashbacks, nightmares, eating disorders, and the list goes on. I was one of them. Are you?

A common thought process is you're stuck with the pain and side effects. I beg to differ. I was a child who carried wounds into adulthood. I didn't understand my behavior. I didn't understand trauma. I had no idea how to be different, but I didn't want to stay miserable. I believe misery is a choice. I pursued the healing and freedom I desired until I found it.

It was a long process. Everyone's process will vary because trauma is personal. There are commonalities we'll cover in a later chapter; but, it's important to remember your healing is yours to own because *Trauma is personal. It does not disappear if it is not validated. When it is ignored or invalidated, the silent screams continue internally heard only by the one held captive. When someone enters the pain and hears the screams healing can begin.*[7]

Do you want to be healed? Do you want to stop feeling miserable? You'll need to take courage to enter your pain and listen to yourself to begin to heal.

Healing is possible, and it takes courage to own it.

OWN YOUR VOICE: NEEDS CAN ONLY BE MET WHEN EXPRESSED

Having needs is not evidence of weakness – it is human.

—Danielle Bernock

Being a human isn't a weakness, and having needs is normal. I learned this valuable lesson through counseling while writing my first book. It sounds silly to me now. But it didn't when I first learned it. If you've suffered your voice being silenced and your needs disregarded, it's not silly to you either. It's oxygen to your soul.

Allowing ourselves to have needs is one step. To have those needs met, someone needs to know. This is accomplished by taking ownership of your voice and speaking up. This can be terribly difficult if you've never done it, but it's possible, and you're worth it.

The title of this book is *Because You Matter*. This truth will change your life once you really believe it. We only take care of things we feel have value. Have you ever spoken up for a friend's needs? Your child's needs? Anyone else's needs? I used to marvel at how I could do that so easily. I ascribed value to them. I would defend others. It wasn't until I saw my value that I owned my voice. I had to allow myself to have needs. I had to deem myself worthy of having those needs met. If I can, so can you. Why? Because you matter. You matter all by yourself. You matter as part of humanity. We flourish in community. We meet each other's needs. Your needs deserve to be met.

It takes courage to own your voice and express your needs to others.

OWN YOUR VULNERABILITY: SHARING IS EMPOWERING

No man is an island, entire of itself.

—John Donne

We're familiar with that quote and nod our heads in agreement. Still, we can find ourselves living as if it's not true. Why is that? Either pride or fear. Pride says, *"I don't need any help."* Fear says, *"They'll think I'm incompetent and needy."* I've been guilty of both attitudes. By design, we need each other. We're created in the image of God. God lives in an eternal community of three in one, also known as the Trinity. Yet, He wanted more and created us.

Making ourselves vulnerable to build a relationship or convey our needs is scary. Questions arise, like *What if they think I'm stupid, or weak or…? What if they don't care? What if they judge me?* But sharing is empowering. There's no depth of relationship without risk. Vulnerability is the only way to build connections. It's the only way to convey our needs to others. One of our basic needs is to be seen. Two of the biggest obstacles to having our needs met are fear and shame. They drive us into hiding. When we emotionally hide, we're not allowing ourselves to be seen. We deny ourselves one of our needs, creating more internal pain. When we're in this state, we need to own our vulnerability and share with someone safe. We need to use wisdom. There's such a thing as sharing too much—or too much too soon. When you own your vulnerability, calculate your risk. Will sharing empower You? Will it empower the hearer? Will it build the relationship? Will your need be met?

I had to own vulnerability with my first book. I calculated the risk of sharing so many intimate things of my life. I was terrified to share. This was going out into the whole world, not just a few people. I was afraid of potential judgment. More than that, I calculated how I could help others and deemed it worth the risk. It was. I've received so much positive feedback. I've helped people. My courage has increased because of it. Our stories can empower others. We need to know we're not alone and there's hope. Our stories remind us no one's perfect. Sharing them is important.

I shared on my website how I felt like hiding and what made me feel like that. The week before I'd been on an emotional rollercoaster of elation, frustration, relief, sorrow, stress, disappointment, anxiety, fear, and anger caused by circumstances beyond my control and the results of choices I made. In my struggle, I ranted about how I felt like I'd failed in the faith department because I'd gotten sick. The Bible tells us *Jesus took our sicknesses* and I believe that. I've received healing using my faith many times. But my body wasn't reflecting what I believed and I didn't understand why. I felt ashamed and wanted to hide. Knowing shame and hiding are destructive, I fought against them. I prayed and read a couple of my own articles, reminding myself that it's ok not to be ok and faith is not magic. I knew this, but I can be so hard on myself. I needed the reminder. Sharing my struggles helped me to come out of hiding by owning the risk of judgment as I made myself vulnerable to my readers. Granted, I was still new to blogging with a small readership, so my risk was low. But owning vulnerability isn't about the size of the audience. It's about feeling naked and hoping to be met with empathy instead of judgment. I asked my readers if they ever felt like hiding. I got a resounding, yes. I talked about how it's shame that drives us into hiding, telling us we don't deserve to be seen, known or loved. Shame is a liar. We are worthy of love. *You* are worthy of love!

According to the story of creation,[8] shame entered our world via a poor choice made by two people who believed a lie. The lie said God was holding out on them, they were incomplete, and they needed to go rogue to gain what they lacked. The truth was they didn't lack anything. They were already complete. It was going rogue that caused separation and disconnection leaving them incomplete. When the one who made them complete in Him from the start (God) came to visit them, Adam and Eve hid in shame, afraid to connect. But God, who'd made Himself vulnerable by creating mankind, met them with empathy. He coaxed them out of hiding and met their need. He covered their nakedness because He's love and *"love covers a multitude of sins."*

We were created for love, connection, and belonging. They're basic human needs. When they're unmet, we feel the pain of disconnection and aloneness. That's why we secretly desire to be found when we hide. But our desire is afraid: *"What if no one notices I'm hiding? What if no one comes looking? What if no one cares? What if I really am all alone?"*

As you own your vulnerability, your needs can be met. Vulnerability picks up courage and takes the risk to be seen. Sometimes it's as simple as admitting something to yourself. (Yes, we humans try to hide things from ourselves. You're not the only one who does this.) Other times it may be a bigger and broader issue where we need to talk with someone else, but not just anyone. It needs to be someone you have reason to trust; for example, a friend, counselor, or God. Trust is important because vulnerability needs empathy. Empathy connects. Empathy says, *"I understand. I feel you. I've been there. I've felt that. It's normal."* It tells you that you're not alone in your normal human condition, you have value, and are loved. This validation gives you the courage to risk vulnerability and come out of hiding the next time.

Every time we take the risk and are met with empathy, our sharing binds us closer together, and our courage grows stronger. That's the power in sharing, which is an exchange within the circle of love empowering us to live loved. The Bible tells us *"two are better than one because the friend helps the other when they fall."* God created man to increase His circle of love. He said it wasn't good for man to be alone so He created Eve for a companion—one who would be one with Adam. When man broke the connection, God risked vulnerability again. Jesus repaired the break in the circle of love inviting us to be one with Him. Sharing is love in action.

Owning your vulnerability is a courageous act with countless benefits.

OWN THE RISK OF TAKING ACTION TO GROW

Life is either a daring adventure or nothing at all.

—Helen Keller

When we're unhappy with something in our life, or where we are in life, we can to do something to change it. That involves risk. We're familiar with where we are now. There's comfort because of familiarity. It's what we have. It's what we know. Change will only happen when we own the risk it takes to grow. This is yet another thing I learned while writing my first book.

I began writing to share my growth. I'd been through a lot. I'd changed a lot and grown. I was so thankful for all the change and growth I felt a responsibility to share, but it was scary, and there were risks. I related to four guys in the Bible who were lepers.[9]

A famine was going on in their city due to their enemies, and they were sitting outside the city gate, discussing their situation and options. They saw themselves in a pickle. If they stayed where they were, they'd die of starvation, but if they acted on their idea to find food they might be killed by the enemy. Staying, they'd die for sure. Taking action was risky, but at least they had a chance.

They took courage and owned the risk. They acted on their idea and discovered the enemy's camp abandoned, full of provisions and gorged themselves. The risk paid off.

Then they felt the responsibility to share this abundance with their countrymen who were still starving, but they were lepers. Lepers weren't allowed to be around healthy people. They owned their risk again and said: *"Let's go at once and report this to the royal palace."*

Their actions ended the siege.

I knew I needed to do the same thing. Take the risk to share. I wanted to *end the siege* of pain and powerlessness in other people's lives. It was scary. But I took courage and owned the risk to share the growth I'd been through, first by writing my book, and then again by publishing it.

My actions not only helped others but also caused more growth in me. I hadn't expected that. I understood we can always grow, and no one's ever *arrived,* but I had no idea how much more there was. Every step took courage and had risks, but every step also grew the courage to take the next risk. This caused continuous growth.

- Because I grew, I wrote my book.
- Because I wrote my book, I grew.
- Because I grew, I published it.
- Because I published it, I grew.
- Because I grew, I continued to share and take more risks causing more growth.

Through this progression, I've developed a greater passion to learn and grow constantly. Taking calculated risks is part of the growth process. We can become so familiar with our current life situations—good and bad—we're blinded to the possibilities available. Every day is a new opportunity for the adventure to learn and grow, but it's something we do on purpose. We don't grow by accident.

By courageously taking risks we can have new growth.

OWN YOUR POWER TO BEGIN AGAIN

Nunc coepi! Now I begin!

—St Josemaría

Whenever you find yourself disappointed in yourself, or angry at something you did—or failed to do—you can pause, learn from it and begin again. You can do this at any time. You don't need to wait for a certain day or a new year. You can do it as soon as *now*. Ask yourself *"Who do I want to be? What change do I desire?"* You have the power inside you for change. The same sun that melts wax hardens clay.[10] The power's in your choice of how to respond. You can quit, or you can get up, dust yourself off and begin again. It takes courage to begin again, but there's power available in your choice. Free choice is a God-given power. If you're feeling defeated, please don't give up. You're not alone. Grab hold of your courage, use your power to choose and dare to begin again.

In addition to your power of choice, you can tap into the power of God. He says when we're weak if we'll lean on Him, He'll make us strong. He'll provide the power we need to begin again. God will help you, not only to begin again, but also apply what you learned from your *"failure."* This will build a new mindset in you called a growth mindset.

Every time you choose to begin again like this, you'll have greater confidence for success and growth. And when you make a mistake or fail again—which will happen because you're human—you can choose to begin again over and over. This is a powerful thing to own.

The power to begin again is available any time you choose.

KEY POINTS

- Courage sees, feels and recognizes the fear or obstacle. It then digs in its heels pushing forward to accomplish your goal.
- Spiritual fear loses its power when we know and believe God's love for us.
- A new life awaits you through courageous new thinking.
- Healing is possible and it takes courage to own it.
- It takes courage to own your voice and express your needs to others.
- Owning your vulnerability is a courageous act with countless benefits.
- By courageously taking risks we can have new growth.
- Whenever you find yourself disappointed in yourself, or angry at something you did—or failed to do—you can pause, learn from it and begin again.

YOU CAN ASK GOD FOR HELP

God, the Bible tells us to not be afraid but to be strong and courageous. I can't do that without you. Please help me. Cause your love to drive fear out of me and make me strong.

NOTES

How Sylvia Took Ownership Of Her Life

...because you've gone through something, find a way, a healthy way to get through it instead of an unhealthy way.

—Sylvia Hubbard

Sylvia is one of the most resilient people I've ever met. We became acquainted at the Rochester Writer's 2019 Spring conference where she was the keynote speaker. I asked to interview her for this book after hearing how she lost everything in a house fire and rebuilt her life.

She took ownership of her life when the fire happened, but the power within her to do so originated from a decision she made after her eighth-grade graduation.

Sylvia's ability to rise above the trauma she endured at the tender age of fourteen amazed me. I had no such inner strength when I was her age. Something we share though is having craved the love of our dad and going without that need being met. In Sylvia's case she told me about how hard she worked in her eighth-grade year to earn the approval and respect of her father.

Her plan was to earn excellent grades, multiple awards, and certificates to be presented at the graduation for her dad to see. Over and over before graduation day came, she'd remind him *"my eighth-grade graduation is coming up"*. Her hungry child heart drew pictures in her mind of her dad's glowing face *"saying, wow, look, she's being called on stage all these times and people are recognizing her and saying what awesome person like this person is."*

She couldn't wait to experience the great day she planned. But it didn't go that way. He didn't show up for the ceremony and her tenacious hope continued. Standing outside after everyone else left she waited, making excuses for him *"maybe he was running late."* For over two hours she waited alone in the dark. He never showed. She started to walk home carrying the evidence she'd gathered to convince her father she mattered crying *"why? why didn't he come for me?"* Devasted she fell on the railroad track, tearing her stockings and sobbed *"I tried, I tried to be the best that I could be for him."*

Her innate resilience stood her to her feet. Her heart took ownership of her value declaring she'd never be a people pleaser again. She decided she was going to be better for herself, not dependent on anyone else's opinion. When she got home her father yelled at her for coming home late and berated her. Her "evidence" meant nothing to him. As she laid in her bed that night, she reaffirmed her decision. This was her life and she would be living it for Sylvia.

That decision saved her fifteen years of grief. It wasn't just her dad. There were multiple bullies tearing her down. But she developed a way to process the trauma she went through.

How Sylvia dealt with her pain was through writing and storytelling. Her mom is who she credits for teaching her the art of storytelling. When Sylvia was little, she lied to her mother frequently and was disciplined for it. In addition to *"a butt whopping"* Sylvia had writing assignments regarding the lies. Through this she fell in love with writing, how words grow into worlds and how good stories move people. Her writing became her *"superpower"* as she took in the pain she endured, owned it and then released it on paper. As she powerfully put it:

"Release it in your stories, you got to take that pain, and you got to remember it because when you put it on paper, that's when

you're putting the power down and releasing it. You're getting it out of you and using it. You're using it for good for someone else."

Such resilience. Taking the pain and repackaging it to help others. Sylvia has been doing this for years. She has independently published forty books. Yes, forty. To Sylvia this is nothing. It's just what she does. But the rest of us are amazed.

It's so interesting how Sylvia doesn't understand our amazement and we don't understand how she could write forty books effortlessly. But it was work, good work, and therapeutic. It's her superpower at work owning who she is because she knows she matters. She knows that stories matter and that sharing them is important. Through our stories we impact one another and alter the course of each other's lives. This is why Sylvia encourages others to write their stories.

"I tell people to tell your story. I mean, it may sound like the craziest story in the whole world, but you never know how that story is going to help others."

Fifteen years after the trauma with her dad and her life altering decision, something amazing happened. She had an interview to attend out in White Lake, Michigan about her work in the community and her car broke down. Needing a ride, she did something she never did—she asked her dad. It was a big ask. It was an hour drive each way plus she would need him to stay during the interview to drive her home. Reluctantly he agreed to. The interview went great. Afterward while Sylvia went to the bathroom the lady who interviewed her went off on her dad about how amazing Sylvia is, and how proud he must be, listing all the wonderful things she's done. He was polite and thanked her. But after, in the car, he turned to Sylvia and for the first time he *saw* her, and he spoke.

"You're really good daughter. You've done some really good stuff. And I'm proud of you."

Wow. Wow. After fifteen years the validation she craved so badly at fourteen came from his lips. Sylvia said it felt great, but she didn't need it anymore because she owned who she was. As a young teenager she'd taken ownership of who she was and what she would become. If she hadn't, she would've spent those fifteen years *"groveling and making him responsible for every bad decision"* she made in her life. Instead, she became a better person for herself and not anybody else.

Suffering happens to all of us. How we respond determines the course of our lives. We can choose to learn and make use of the pain like Sylvia did instead of making excuses that allow our pain to hurt others. Life is only so long. Sylvia talked about how brief our lives are and how every moment matters. Making use of every moment is important.

Then a moment happened when Sylvia had another opportunity to take ownership.

"Yeah, when the fire happened, it was kind of like, What the h . . . what the crap. What did I do to deserve this?"

Sylvia's home burned to the ground. She and her children escaped with their lives. Questions and emotions raged in her soul with the force of a freight train. She had been at a comfortable place, working hard, doing the best she could. It didn't make sense. Her son voiced how she did so much for so many. They felt undeserved punishment.

That's what trauma does; it cuts to the fiber of your being.

"And that's really scary when your spirituality is being challenged like this. That really takes you to another place where you start to question everything that you have ever done."

But the resilience she built through the choice she made as a youth empowered her to take ownership and start working her way through. Sylvia was tenacious. She refused the victim mindset to sit around waiting for grants to help. It's a good thing because organizations didn't contact her offering to help for four months. By then she was already working on her new home with Habitat for Humanity. And that is how Sylvia is. If something doesn't go right, she moves in another direction, and if that doesn't work, she'll move in a different direction again, because she knows her value.

Knowing your value is vital. It drives our life purpose. When we look at all the things Sylvia has accomplished and is still doing, we see how her ownership of her value has propelled her. It's where she says she gets her strength, courage and tenacity. Because she takes ownership of her value, she owns the circumstances in her life and chooses to move forward.

Sylvia carries a strong sense of community. Helping others is part of who she is and the message she spreads. She encourages others to put value in themselves when things aren't going according to plan. And if that doesn't work then to help someone else. Helping others will help you. *"They become better then you become better."*

Sylvia wants everyone to take this kind of ownership. It grieves her when people come to her saying they can't do something because of someone else. If you're feeling held back like that, ask yourself these three questions Sylvia offers:

1. Is this person paying your bills?
2. Did this person breathe life into you: Are they some type of God or something?
3. Why are you allowing someone to take away your happiness at all?

"Stop worrying about what other people are going to think or what other people are going to say. You are blocking your blessings in life when you decide to let other people dictate over you what you should be doing or what is meant for you to do."

Because Sylvia did this, in addition to her books, she's the founder of Motown Writers and Michigan Literary Network. Don't defer your life to someone else. Do what's in your heart.

Find out more about Sylvia and what she has to offer in the endnotes.

CHAPTER 6

Owning Your Mess

I'm the mess. Sometimes I'm the broom. On the hardest days, I have to be both.

—Rudy Francisco

HOW TO BEGIN

No one has a perfect life. We might think other people have everything together but it's not true. We only see the edited version. Everyone has some sort of mess going on in their life. Realizing this helps us to take ownership of our own messes without shame. As we move into this next chapter remember your immense value and grab ahold of your courage because it can be difficult to look deep within ourselves. But doing this is the beginning of freedom because we cannot address what we refuse to own.

I dare you to own your mess and receive help and healing.

OWN THE CHAOS: SEEING IS THE BEGINNING OF FREEDOM

You can't heal what you don't acknowledge.

—Jack Canfield

I started to write a book a couple years ago but ended up setting it aside. It began with owning the messy emotions I'd not been dealing with well and how I realized something had to change.

The mess of my emotions exploded through an epic meltdown. I'll share more about this life-changing meltdown later. For now, I want to point out I had a choice when this meltdown invaded my life. I could own the chaos that had caused it and do something, or do nothing and pretend it would go away on its own. Owning it and taking action would be no small task. It would be a lot of emotional and mental hard work. I chose the work because I knew it was the only way to freedom. Doing nothing would be my refusal to see the chaos in my life. My emotions were a mess. There were several reasons, and I needed to look at each and every one of them and address them all.

Because I'd learned I mattered, I took courage and owned the chaos. I looked at the mess on my insides and saw they were leaking into my life, confirming my need for change.

Knowing you matter gives you the courage to own the chaos in your life.

OWN YOUR REALITY: NO MALICE ≠ NO HARM

The scars you can't see are the hardest to heal.

—Astrid Alauda

When a person has suffered harm it's easy to believe there was malicious intent, especially if the harm is deeply traumatic. The two seem to go together. I learned that's not always true. Gaining this understanding was an important part of my healing process. I suffered harm from diverse sources. Deep soul wounds affected me well into adulthood. I knew the source of some. Others, I didn't. It wasn't until I began writing my story with the support of my counselor that they came to light. She helped me uncover hidden traumas where the harm had no malicious intent. When I casually brought them up her words were *"Something went terribly wrong."* It was eye-opening.

I knew the bullies were malicious. That was obvious. Perhaps they didn't understand malice, being kids themselves. However, their actions were intentional.

Then there were others who were ignorant or perhaps misguided. My first-grade teacher, for example, who used shame as a tool in the classroom. There are still *"educators"* using shame as a tool. It's not. It's harmful. It's manipulative, controlling, and wrong. Shame is never good.

I doubt the leaders of the church who delivered the bullseye trauma to my soul were intentionally malicious. I think they were misguided by false beliefs. Maybe pride. I don't know; but, I don't think their intention was to cause the deep trauma that kept me from believing God loved me, even though it's what happened.

Then there were my parents. Imperfect humans simply making mistakes—no malice, yet I was harmed. This was the hardest thing for me to own. I had to own the reality of harm even when there was no malice. The two had to be separated. Malice is an intention while harm is a result. Harm isn't measured by malice. Although I suffered trauma inflicted maliciously by some, other trauma happened accidentally.

Do you have harm without malice in your life? Have you negated the harm because *"they didn't mean it?"* This doesn't make the harm disappear. If it's true, own your reality. You don't need to blame. You need to heal.

By owning the reality that No Malice ≠ No Harm you can forgive others and begin healing.

OWN THE TRUTH: VALIDATION IS THE BEGINNING OF FREEDOM

Trauma is personal. It does not disappear if it is not validated. When it is ignored or invalidated the silent screams continue internally heard only by the one held captive. When someone enters the pain and hears the screams healing can begin.

—Danielle Bernock

We can be harmed in many ways. Physically, emotionally, mentally, financially, relationally, etc.; and there are varying depths it can affect us. What kind of harm have you sustained? How deeply it impacts and effects your everyday life is where you'll find the answer.

Consider the following questions seriously.

Do you get annoyed for apparently no reason? Do you have perpetual internal chaos? Are you passive-aggressive? Do you feel like you have no control over your life? Do you live behind a mask, being who you think people want you to be? Do you suffer from being emotionally triggered? Do you have significant pieces of your childhood missing from your memory? Do you avoid relationships? Do you have self-harming behaviors?

Those are just some of the various symptoms of childhood and emotional trauma. They're evidence of a problem that won't go away without healing. Trauma can cause us to hide due to feelings of shame. Shame and pain like darkness. They fester and grow there. Pain is only good as an indicator there's a problem. Shame is never good. Living in either is not living well. It's miserable. To heal takes light. The light of truth. Shame hates the light. It fears the light. Shame knows the light will destroy it. Truth is the path to freedom. Seeing and then acknowledging it is called validation.

Validation is the beginning of freedom. You can't heal from trauma if you won't call it what it is. Dismissing trauma in your life as not important gives it the power to bind you. Do you have the symptoms of trauma at work in your life? If the answer is yes, take courage and admit the truth.

Trauma isn't one size fits all and the causes are diverse. *Trauma is personal* was a deep and profound revelation to me. I discovered how true it was even more by the overwhelming way those words resonated with others. I learned it doesn't matter if someone else thinks what happened to me was traumatic or not. It's personal. It's my life. If I was traumatized, I was traumatized. It's as simple as that. Likewise, if you were traumatized, you were traumatized. That's the truth to own.

I was traumatized by things I negated and dismissed for different reasons. It wasn't until I called it what it was that healing began. Validation doesn't heal it. Validation is the first step. Then there's work. But it's good work that brings freedom and healing and the ability to live well.

If it's true you've suffered trauma, I dare you to own that truth.

OWN YOUR TRAUMA: SMALL THINGS ARE BIG WHEN STRATEGICALLY PLACED

Trauma is perhaps the most avoided, ignored, belittled, denied, misunderstood, and untreated cause of human suffering.

—Peter Levine

I suffered from childhood trauma. I spent years denying the trauma that plagued me. It was trivial to me for reasons hidden within the trauma itself. The door to my healing opened with validation but I had to walk through the door and own what had traumatized me. Owning your trauma can sound awful, but it's an important step on your pathway to healing and a new life. Understanding that trauma is personal is crucial. It's not the size of the incident that determined its effect on you. It's how you received/perceived it.

Trauma is not an event. Trauma is an effect. There are people who go through major disasters with little effect and those who are devasted, as well as a range in the middle. Trauma isn't a circumstance, incident, or disaster. Those things happen around us. Trauma occurs inside us.

I was traumatized as a child by a succession of things. Some things were hidden by me in fear or shame. Others were dismissed as trivial when they happened to me. Because of this, I believed they were no big deal and I was the one with the problem. But that was a lie. These *"small things"* worked together in a strategic way to devastate my soul.

For example, if someone wants to destroy a skyscraper there are certain requirements. They don't just throw a bomb in there. That's messy and inefficient. The best way to destroy a skyscraper is to level it using a technique called implosion.[11] To implode a building takes a lot of time to plan the proper strategy. Without the precision required of where to put the explosives and when to set them off, gravity can't pull the building straight down flat. This method safely levels the building so its destruction doesn't harm anything around it. If destruction can be beautiful, this is a visual.

I learned it wasn't simply the circumstances I went through that traumatized me. It was when and how and in what order. It was like the strategic placing and timing of explosive material for a building implosion.

Whatever happened in your soul is what needs to be owned. It doesn't matter if the circumstance surrounding it seems big or small. What happened inside you is what happened inside you. Belittling or denying it won't make it go away. It'll make it fester. It'll make you miserable. Evidence shows it can shorten your life. Again, it doesn't matter what caused the trauma, it needs to be owned to be healed. Please do this, because you matter.

To heal I had to own the truth I was traumatized by my first-grade teacher. I never told anyone about the incident when it happened. Shame got involved and I hid. Shame would've kept it a secret forever, dismissing it as *no big deal*. But when the trauma was triggered by what should've been a harmless joke, turning me into an emotional wreck, I said *this has to stop*. I took possession of the trauma and cried out to God for help. My wound was complex. He helped me dismantle it and showed me what the internal voice of pain was saying. It was the voice of shame telling me I didn't matter. Shame lies. The Spirit of Grace replaced the lies with truth. The truth is the trauma was undeserved and was not my fault. What I needed was love. Loves says I matter. Those two words "*I matter*" became a tool for my healing. I suffered from that specific trauma in multiple ways for forty-six years. Not anymore. That was the last time I was triggered back to that incident in first grade because the trauma in my soul has been healed. It took owning the truth and refusing the lies of shame for me to be healed.

Dismantle your trauma instead of discounting it so you can heal.

OWN YOUR DYSFUNCTION: NO ONE'S CHILDHOOD IS PERFECT

My childhood is a part of my story, and it's why I'm who I am today and why my career is what it is.

—Misty Copeland

As a child growing up, I looked at certain other children and wished for their lives, sometimes wishing I were them. They seemed to have it all together while I felt so inferior. After addressing the trauma and dysfunction in my life, I understand how wrong my perception was. No one has a perfect childhood. Granted not all children suffer trauma. And there are those with less dysfunction than others. But because we're all human we can never be rid of dysfunction. People make mistakes and we hurt one another by accident. Remember the section No Malice ≠ No Harm.

Taking a good look at and dealing with whatever dysfunction there was in your childhood is owning it. By owning it you empower yourself to live past it and break free of its power to affect you. Owning your dysfunction teaches you. It gives you the ability to choose how to go forward. Shine the light of truth on it. Add in some grace for all family members because they're human. Forgive and draw boundaries where needed. Make changes where needed. Do your best and continue to grow. Then keep doing your best. We can lessen dysfunction by doing this.

I made mistakes in raising my kids. Our family had our own flavor of dysfunction. I did the best I knew how, yet I'd do things differently now because I've grown and changed. But I don't have a time machine. I've told my children although I didn't do everything perfectly, I improved on my parenting from my parents, and they won't be perfect either but are improving on my parenting.

The opposite of owning your dysfunction is to blame. Living in blame makes you a powerless victim. There's a song by Kelly Clarkson called *Because of You*. This song helped me shift the *cause* of my pain from myself to other people. I needed to know this truth: children are *not* to blame for their trauma. Blame, as in identifying the cause, is useful. After that, the focus needs to shift to healing the wound it caused. We need to separate the human that's guilty of an action from the action itself, and change our focus to how the action or actions affected our soul.

- *Be-cause.*
- There was a cause.
- There was an effect.

Healing comes into view when blame transforms into a cause, instead of judgment. Judgment and blame become useless *because* the past can't be changed. What happened cannot unhappen. The cause can't be removed but the effect can be healed.

Acknowledging dysfunction can move you from victim to survivor to victor.

OWN YOUR LOSS: WE CAN'T HAVE WHAT NEVER WAS

He heals the brokenhearted and binds up their wounds.
—David

Longing for something you can't have is terribly painful. Especially for something impossible. For example, if you wish you were taller, or you wish you were born in a different country, family or time in history; or, you wish your childhood were different. To continue to wish for something you have no power to change is to allow yourself to live in misery. The only way back to joy is to own the loss. Let it go and count it lost. Grieve over it, and then you'll be able to move past it as I did.

I suffered horribly from what we call daddy issues. They come from all kinds of reasons/situations/experiences or lack thereof. What caused mine are in *Emerging With Wings*, but more importantly, is how I overcame. It was a process that began with a revelation. I longed for what never was. I wanted what could not be. This revelation came through my counselor during a session. We were talking about my dad. She asked how I saw him and "Without hesitation I said 'a mirage. He was there but not there.'"[12] To my surprise, she validated my perspective. That hadn't happened before. We continued to talk and the thing I yearned for took on words. I longed for a relationship with my dad. However, that's not possible because he died long before. Her words were hard to hear, but oh so true. "She said I had a hole and had grown around it. But it can never be removed. What was not, cannot become – my dad is gone. The love was wanting and cannot be obtained . . . there is only loss. Loss not only of my dad, but I must grieve and let go of the dad I wish I had but never did. There is only going forward."[13] I had to own the loss. I had to accept the truth. I had to validate my feelings by mourning, and then let them go. Once I finally did, the misery ended. This is walking through.

Grieving is an important part of accepting loss and healing.

OWN YOUR GRIEF: DEATH DEVASTATES

Blessed are those who mourn, for they will be comforted.

—Jesus

Death is a strange thing. When anyone encounters it there's always an effect. Although death is a part of life on planet earth, we instinctively know there's something wrong with it. Death devastates the soul because we were designed to live eternally. Every time we encounter death it reminds us that we don't hold the power of life and death. It makes the natural world around us feel fragile and unsafe. For example, I remember going with my mother to check on an elderly neighbor when I was young. It was late in the morning and her picture window curtains were closed. Her daily signal she was up and about was to open them. We knocked on her door, but she didn't answer. My mother used her key to let us in. We found her on the floor in the hallway—dead. I wasn't close to her so I didn't feel grief at the loss of a relationship. What I did feel was a void, an emptiness—a vacuum—from being in the presence of her dead body. That awful feeling followed me home. Where there was supposed to be life was death and I didn't know how to handle it. Children have a more difficult time dealing with death. It's unsettling to their world. They don't understand what grief is.

Grief is a natural response to death. It comes in varying degrees and can be quite complicated depending on who the person was in your life, and the situation surrounding the death, or deaths. For example, it could be a family member who died of cancer; a public figure like the assassination of John F. Kennedy or John Lennon; the crew of the Challenger space shuttle that blew up 73 seconds after liftoff; the people who lost their lives in the terror attack on the twin towers in New York City on September 11, 2001; or a friend killed in a car accident. Each of these are different examples. Your response reflects how it impacted you. Owning this response is critical to becoming whole again because it's accepting your reality like we talked about earlier.

Grief is the emotional pain from the wound created when someone or something is torn from your life. Grieving is a passageway. Expressing your grief empowers you to journey through.

Failing to own your grief, builds a prison of pain for your soul.

KEY POINTS

- We might think other people have everything together but it's not true. We only see the edited version.
- Knowing you matter gives you the courage to own the chaos in your life.
- Malice can be absent and soul injury can still occur.
- You can't heal from trauma if you won't call it what it is.
- Trauma isn't a circumstance, incident, or disaster. Those things happen around us. Trauma occurs inside us.
- What happened inside you is what happened inside you. Belittling or denying it won't make it go away.
- Healing comes into view when blame transforms into a cause, instead of judgment.
- Grieving is a passageway. Expressing your grief empowers you to journey through.

YOU CAN ASK GOD FOR HELP

God, help me take ownership of the messes in my life and hand them to you. Help me to see what I need to see so I can do that. Lead me down the path of healing. Help me mourn the losses in my life and heal my soul.

NOTES

How Randy Took Ownership Of His Life

They didn't call it PTSD then. But it's really what it was, where I just blocked out of all the pain of the trauma.

—Randy Arwine

I met Randy many years ago. He worked with my husband in the automotive industry until 2010. His choice to change careers midlife along with a diagnosis he didn't allow to sideline him is what led me to ask for an interview. Randy is a kind and compassionate soul with a quiet inner strength helping other men rewrite their life stories. As Randy and I spoke, he revealed two traumas that ran deep and how they silently tried to destroy him.

The first one took place on Sunday the fourteenth of October in 1984. A night many celebrated as the Detroit Tigers won the World Series. But it wasn't a night for Randy, or his wife, to celebrate. It was a night that would live in infamy causing unimaginable pain. That night their collective best friend, best man at their wedding, was murdered.

Can you imagine? I can't. I don't really want to. The thought of it's painful enough. Such loss. But the loss grew worse as the trauma derailed their lives. Kathy (Randy's wife) was pregnant with their first child and once again it should have been a time for celebration. He was going to be a daddy to a little girl. They named her Kerrie. But the grief cast a huge shadow.

"That derailed both of us. Pretty much I . . . I pretty much blocked out most of 1985. I don't remember a whole lot of it. I remember Kerrie being born. I remember sometime in 85 'Look, I *got a promotion at work.' I don't remember a whole lot until the following fall when the colors started changing."*

By the fall of 1985 Kathy had processed her grief but Randy hadn't. She made a counseling appointment for him to begin to unpack the trauma. He was a mess and didn't know it. Kathy knew it well. Too well and knew it had to stop. Something had to be done. Side effects of the trauma in his soul prevented him from processing normal conversation. It was through this misunderstood conversation Randy got his epiphany that he needed help.

"I realized that when Kathy told me to go to counseling.

What I heard was—we had a counseling appointment, and that we're going to go over her mom's for dinner afterwards.

What she actually said was—you have a counseling appointment and if you don't go, I'm taking our daughter and I'm moving back in with my mom and dad. That's how out of it I was. So, I realized, once I finally understood that, that something was wrong."

Randy took ownership of his grief once he saw what it was doing to his life and went to counseling. He went all in.

"I found a counselor that understood that struggle, and she really helped both of us understand what was going on."

He was dealing with PTSD even though they didn't call it that back then. PTSD used to be associated only with war, but psychologists know better now. Post-Traumatic Stress Disorder is not defined by a preceding event, it's the aftereffects of severe emotional trauma.

As Randy was in counseling the other deep trauma came to light. The one from his childhood he'd dismissed as "normal". But it was leaking into his life and Kathy was paying the price. This isn't uncommon. When children are traumatized, they don't know normal from unnormal because the trauma is their normal. But trauma isn't normal. Trauma is personal and deeply destructive.

Randy grew up in an alcoholic home where a child must be careful of everything they say because *"you're not allowed to speak the truth."* Randy didn't know what to think about who he was or who he was going to become. He was the second oldest of four children and small for his age. Because of his lack of stature Randy felt his dad was ashamed of him. Fear, shame, and distrust led him into fistfights because of the story he told himself about himself.

"I thought . . . I thought it was normal. I just thought that that's just the way it was. And, you know, I realized that that shame, isolated, disconnected me from not only myself, but from others as well. I didn't know how . . . I didn't know then at all, how deeply it was impacting me."

Shame is destructive. I've written about this before. When I wrote about how shame is never good, I got flack. I stand my ground—shame is never good. Had Randy not taken ownership of the shame that was ruining his life he wouldn't be the man he is today. A man changing the lives of other men.

"Understanding that shame, the shame of growing up in a home that's shame based, where you feel paralyzed, to make decisions to do anything different than what the collective family members want, impacted me far more than I realized growing up."

It was in counseling that Randy began to learn how to live differently. When he started addressing his childhood he thought looking into codependency and enmeshment was the way for him to deal with it. And that is the way for some. But his counselor led him in a different direction. She gave him a book on how to become a better husband and he accepted it.

This is when the two things I'd interviewed Randy for in the first place came into the story. At forty-eight years old he was diagnosed with Multiple Sclerosis commonly referred to as MS. It's rare for a man that old to be given the diagnosis.

Trauma is a sucker punch to our sense of control and Randy's diagnosis did just that. Questions without answers made him emotionally dizzy until two things happened.

"A young woman prophesied over me, she prayed for healing...and spoke to me things that God was saying to me and that I was saying to God. That no one else knew. And that's when I realized, okay, this is serious. This is real. And I need to take it serious. I need to really trust God in the direction that He was taking me."

Right after that Randy met a group of guys. These men helped him process the traumas in his life and find purpose in a new and unique way. It was at something called a *"story weekend"*—a retreat to help men *"connect the dots in their lives"*. Going on this retreat dramatically changed Randy's life. These newfound friends saw in him what many had seen for years. They began a journey together helping Randy to see what was so obvious to everyone else.

"I was always told growing up and through other people that I should go into counseling. Because people listen to me. That I have a good listening ear and I care about people. I never really took that serious."

Randy began to see his gifts, was invited to help with the retreats and started working toward a counseling degree. Two years later Awakened Heart Ministries was born, and he was on their board of directors. He continued his studies and graduated with a degree in Christian counseling in 2007 for the purpose of helping others. The following year the automotive world started to struggle. His employer wanted him to travel to third world countries and he couldn't bring himself to do it because of the MS.

"I didn't want to end up in a third world hospital, because it was kind of scary."

When the housing market crashed in 2008 the automotive industry suffered as well. Randy was laid off in July of 2009. For fifteen months he searched for work, struggling emotionally but leaning hard into his faith. God showed up in miraculous ways providing for him and his family. He remembered what the young woman prophesied over him years before about his desires and having a bigger story. During this time the staff at AHM were praying about bringing him on staff. In 2010 they offered Randy a full-time position.

"I said goodbye to the automotive field. And they've tried to hire me back three times since then. And I tell them the same thing every time. I like getting up in the morning now."

Now Randy is the Director of Community and Discipleship at Awakened Heart Ministries. Through taking ownership of what kind of a man he wanted to be Randy refused to allow MS to make him a victim. Instead he chose to find a purpose and is writing the end of his story in faith and courage.

"I've talked to a lot of people with the MS diagnosis that really, they don't have God in their life, they feel really victimized. And I realized that despite the circumstances of you know, my health in this world God still created me for something and I wanted to move towards that as opposed to wallow in the self-pity."

At AHM, Randy mentors men one on one and in groups. He helps them take ownership of their lives and see hidden barriers that prevent them from moving forward. Through story venues the men are able to *"see their unique place and purpose in God's larger story"* so they can flourish in their relationships. When I asked Randy where he got his courage and strength to own up to the things in his life, his answer was threefold. His relationship with Christ, his wife and the community of men he has the privilege to work with every day.

"We have a saying. We walk with each other, put our arms around each other and kick each other in the butt when we need it."

It's important to Randy that men understand how powerful they are and the proper use of their power. He teaches them to use their power to create harmony and community so others can flourish also. Getting rid of shame is imperative. Randy is committed to helping men see *"the shame that they deal with doesn't have to be the end of their story. It could be a catalyst for them to take ownership of their own lives. And to be able to use their power the way God has given to them to change the legacy of their families and their kids' families down the road."*

Find out more about Randy and what he has to offer in the endnotes.

CHAPTER 7

Owning Your Pain

Recovery begins with embracing our pain and taking the risk to share it with others.

—John Bradshaw

HOW TO BEGIN

Pain is part of human existence. In our bodies it's what sounds the alarm, telling us there's a problem, so we'll tend to it. Physical, mental and emotional pain are all different yet all need tending to. All need comfort, care, and healing. Still, because mental and emotional pain can't be seen with the eyes, we treat it differently from physical pain. This is an injustice. Unresolved mental and emotional pain leak into our lives, creating a mess. In the previous chapter, we talked about owning our mess. The messes in our lives create pain. To fully own the mess, we need to own the pain that accompanies it.

I dare you to own your pain so you can make use of it.

OWNING YOUR PAIN IS HOW YOU CAN OVERCOME IT.

We must embrace pain and burn it as fuel for our journey.

—Kenji Miyazawa

The pain we feel is ours alone. We can try to pawn it off on someone else using blame. We can try to numb it using various drugs or alcohol. We can shove it down deep invalidating its right to be there. We can fall on our face crying out to God for help when we don't understand it. I've done all of these, but healing didn't come until I did that last one.

Remember me mentioning my epic meltdown? It's time for me to share the story with you. It was the beginning of the book I started but then stopped because I wasn't ready. I still had crap in my life. I had to take ownership of my mess and my pain. The Spirit of Grace helped me do it.

The meltdown seemed to come out of nowhere. It had been a fantastic day. It was the first Christmas we'd all been together in four years. The three *"littles"* were laying on the floor huddled together watching a movie, each of them cozied up inside their new blankets from their Great Gramma earlier that day. We were all engaged in fun and laughter playing games together. Joy and celebration were in order; but, something was wrong.

The next morning, I woke up to flashbacks of the meltdown. It scared me. It was disturbing because all I could remember was melting down but no details. I couldn't remember what it was about. Panic wanted to take over. I remembered who I was with, or at least two people I knew of. I remembered uncontrollably sobbing, and the intense emotion that went with it.

I felt it again.

But I had no recollection of any words. It was even more upsetting because this wasn't my first meltdown in recent times. A pattern seemed to be forming. Shame presented itself. Condemnation immediately followed. Using wordless emotions, they both disdained me. They had reason . . . or at least I thought so. I'd violated my inner vow and had gotten blackout drunk on wine which I believed to be the cause of the meltdown. I was wrong.

Initially, I felt disoriented and dazed as if my internal circuit breaker broke, causing my mental state to go haywire and shut off. In the dark frozen feeling, I surveyed the landscape of my soul for light. Perhaps in hope, or maybe in desperation, but like someone who was lost in the desert looking for water, I didn't like where I was. I didn't like how I felt. I didn't like what I'd done. I didn't know what to do. I'd been here before.

On second thought, no, I hadn't.

In the middle of my internal exploration, I found something. I realized *He* was with me. The Spirit of Grace sat here with me, I was certain of it. Shame and condemnation were still there. His presence didn't require them to leave. It felt extremely odd. It was like the two of them swirled about like smoke, tempting me to internalize and own them as if they were a sweet fragrance to inhale instead of the putrid odor they truly were. I'd done that before, breathed them in accepting their derision, owning them as my identity. Many times. But today was different. This time I knew the Spirit of Grace was not only there with me, but I also noticed He wasn't mad. He wasn't even annoyed! A great portion of my life, I'd held a very negative view of God. I'd seen him as harsh, unpleasable, and mean. Subsequently, I came to know him in a better light but the nagging feeling of *waiting for the other shoe to drop* still lurked in the corners of my soul for a long time. It wasn't until I saw Him as the Spirit of Grace that my perceptions began to change. The word *began,* implies slow development.

The Spirit of Grace *not* being angry with me when I was guilty of doing something I believed to be horribly wrong, was a mindset

I was still getting used to. Apparently, I'd made more progress than I'd thought. On this personally scandalous morning, my perception verified I believed in the Spirit of Grace's unconditional love and forgiveness. As I realized this, I turned to face the shame and condemnation as if they were two people standing there, and simply dismissed them, forcing them to leave. I had the power to do so. I chose to believe that the Spirit of Grace had the perfection I wanted and needed, and He loved me right where I was. I turned to the Spirit of Grace and asked for help. He embraced and comforted me. I felt safe. His comfort reassured me, He's always there to be *with* me, and *for* me, because of how He loves me. I was *not* alone in this mess I had found myself.

After the Spirit of Grace's little love fest, He guided me on what actions would be good to take next and gave me the courage to follow through. First, I needed to call the two people who'd been with me during the meltdown, inquire what had happened, and ask for their help. What a humbling thing to do. *Had I humiliated myself? Would they be angry with me?* Thoughts like these raced through my head as I felt the fear around me. I chose to take hold of the courage the Spirit of Grace provided, and I made the first call.

As planned, I confessed what I'd done, and how I didn't remember. I told her about the flashbacks and what I did remember. I asked her if she would help me and tell me what had happened. She responded graciously and elaborated on what had taken place, and the things I had said. I took notes. I asked her questions and took more notes. I thanked her profusely, and she gently comforted me. The Spirit of Grace was there.

With the second person, I repeated the same course of action and was met with the same compassionate response. She had some different information to share, which I added to my notes. I was in awe of the grace I received and empowered with the hope of change.

I savored the feeling of comfort before taking my next step of action—talking with my husband. He'd never given me any reason to shrink back from talking with him about anything, yet I was afraid. Fear is irrational at times. It doesn't always need a reason. I was disappointed in myself and felt threatened that he would be as well. The fear was wrong as it so often is. Instead of disappointment, he told me he was concerned about me. Concerned, because he knew I had a lot going on, but I didn't seem to be processing it well. I told him he was correct. I went on to tell him how I'd made the phone calls and gathered the information, as well as my responses to the information. I told him I had insight I didn't have before, and this time, I was going to take a different action. I had to learn how to cope more efficiently.

I learned from the two ladies that although my meltdown had numerous parts, there was one central issue. It revolved around my inability to manage colliding extremes of emotions—joy/sorrow, bliss/grief, belonging/isolation, acceptance/rejection, love/fear, connection/separation—all happening at the same time. It was like a bomb went off in my soul, and the excess wine I consumed made a way for it to come out. It was the best meltdown I ever had, and I couldn't have been happier it happened.

Best meltdown ever? How can such a thing be good? Maybe you know. Maybe you've had a *good* one. Maybe not. This was a first for me—not a first meltdown, as I said before, but it was a first for me to call it *good*. Prior to this, I would look at it as a bad thing, a loss of control, a pathetic failure—except for the rare occasion I felt it was warranted, like after a death, or something I considered extreme enough. However, this one was just what I didn't know I needed. This one changed my life. I didn't understand what was going on inside me, and I needed to find out.

We all know stress is part of life, and there are all different kinds. Therefore, it's to our benefit to learn how to handle it in healthy ways. We don't always do that. Sometimes we don't know how, and other times we have too much too fast coming at us like an automatic pitching machine gone haywire.

For a significant amount of time, my life had been booming with emotional stress like a broken pitching machine. Not all of it was bad, so I had a problem labeling it as stress. During this time, I learned how *common* emotional stress is which only made it worse. If it's so common, I expected myself to deal with it effortlessly. I'd learned so much from my counselor, and writing my first book, that I expected more from myself. However, one primary thing I learned was how weak I was in constructive emotional processing. It was a discovery that required validation. I received validation. I addressed what I discovered. However, it's painfully obvious there's more work to be done, new action to be taken.

Thank you, meltdown.

NEW ACTION TO OWN

I had a little awareness of what it was from my love fest with the Spirit of Grace, but I knew there was more. Following His lead, I spent the day researching coping mechanisms, feelings, and emotions, looking for tools to help. I added this information to the words He'd led me to earlier that morning to comfort me. Words from the Bible found in Ecclesiastes 3 and Psalm 31: *"To everything there is a season and a time for every purpose under heaven."* / *"My times are in thy hand: deliver me from the hand of mine enemies, and from them that persecute me."* To oversimplify, I began a process with the Spirit of Grace I fondly referred to as *"What time is it Mr. Fox?"* like the children's game. And that's just like Him, to simplify things in childlike ways. Later that night, I learned these new things were part of a strategy He was providing for me.

The word strategy became important.

The word came from a movie my husband and I rented that night. Yes, a movie. The Spirit of Grace has often used movies to teach me—a wide variety of movies. Some religious people think that's not possible, but their opinions don't stop God. Funny thing is I didn't have much interest in this movie before. It was the movie *War Room*. I didn't know much about it except it was a Christian movie about prayer. In my ignorance, I wasn't fond of the title. I finally had a grasp on the love and grace of God, so why would I want to connect war with prayer? But I was in a place of neediness, and He took this timely opportunity to nudge me to watch it. It became apparent, I knew just enough about this movie to get myself into trouble. How silly we humans can be when we think we know so much but actually know so little. The movie was not what I expected. I took notes during it.

There were three specific quotes that resonated in my heart. The first being *"Victory doesn't come by accident."* With those words, the Spirit of Grace showed me the requirement of being deliberate, premeditated. Wishing things were different was not going to work, nor would being half-assed about it. A strategy is implied in this quote, although it's not stated. The next is, *"Very few of us know how to fight the right way."* He used this one to show me there was a way. If I didn't find it, I wouldn't gain victory. More importantly, if I would find it, learn it and apply it, I would gain victory. He reminded me of how He had taken me down this strategy building road before as well as the victory it brought. More about that later. This quote, like the previous one, doesn't use the word strategy either but implies it. The third quote does. It's *"Somebody has to develop a strategy to combat the enemy."* This quote made the word strategy clear in addition to confirming it was my responsibility to develop said strategy if victory was going to happen. I needed a strategy to handle feelings, especially extremes. The Spirit of Grace had given me the tools I needed to build upon.

And so, it began. My new journey into this land called processing feelings.

Not long into this journey, I discovered there are many who've gone before me as well as those who haven't had the courage to embark, or simply have refused. I found friends and advocates, creatures, and monsters.

Welcome to my world.

About six weeks into my journey, I tamed my first monster.

The monster was an ambiguous swirl of numerous emotions, tormenting at every opportunity. Internal turbulence, instability, and chaos came and went at will. I didn't know what to do with this monster, which was precisely the problem. That's what made it a monster, until the day I miraculously transformed the monster into a manageable creature by the grace of God.

The Spirit of Grace gave me its name. All the way home from visiting my mother-in-law, Ann, the words sang in my heart: *A Bird Named Payn, A Bird Named Payn, A Bird Named Payn.* I didn't understand what the words meant, but I knew they were important. Curious to find out, I felt inclined to sit down at my computer and begin to write. An unusual story flowed from my fingers, bringing insight to my heart, and peace to my mind. It wove together some of the ragged pieces from the night of the meltdown. Pieces that deeply bound my mother-in-law and me together. Pieces validating emotions I'd been dismissing.

My friend, Validation brought sense to the monstrous chaos of emotion, reducing it to a bird confined to its name.

This unusual story is how I owned my complex monstrous pain and processed it.

A BIRD NAMED PAYN[14]

I found her sitting in her wheelchair in the common area of the memory care facility when I arrived. This journey, I walked with my mother-in-law, Ann, had begun many years ago.

The first few years of my marriage, she played a significant role as comforter and refuge for me numerous times. I became pregnant a month after getting married, and my hormones were more than I could handle. One emotionally awful day in my second trimester, I found myself walking the seven miles to her house from the park near where I lived. I often went to this park to swing on the swings for comfort, but it wasn't working. She was surprised by my unannounced arrival and asked how I got there. I told her I'd walked. Although shocked, she greeted me with the hug I so badly needed. I fell apart in sobs, and she held me. That's only one example of how the Spirit of Grace ministered to me through her and bound my soul to hers.

Today I had the privilege of feeding her lunch. She can't do it herself anymore. I pondered *how many lunches had she provided for my family and me?* Too many to count. And then I recalled the countless times she and her late husband fed others with their *free grocery store* they'd set up in their basement for people who needed a helping hand. I'd brought a few of my friends there to shop when they needed it. Yes, feeding her was a privilege and I rejoiced when I was able to get her to eat half a bowl of soup and a bowl of ice cream, as well as drink the two glasses of juice. That's a feast for her now. She's lost over forty-four pounds since *the bird* showed up.

Four years earlier, *the bird* found my mother-in-law. She didn't want it. It didn't care. Her husband had recently passed, and she was moving into a new place because she required assistance she didn't want. The new place was beautiful, and the staff was accepting of her *bird*. They helped her find a cage suitable for it, so it had a place to go instead of circling over her head squawking like a vulture. She grew to love this new place and those entrusted with her care. She knew they loved her also. For a season, there was peace. It seemed *the bird* was mostly caged and covered. However, there were times *the bird* would get out and wreak havoc until it was caught and put away again.

After a few years, *the bird* started getting out more frequently, and it was getting harder to catch and cage it. Many times, uncertainty would cause control to fly out the window. The time came when the bird started to follow me home, occasionally. It would mysteriously circle above my home. I could feel it, but not see it. I didn't know what to do with those monstrous emotions. While my husband was working out of town, we nearly lost my mother-in-law. *The bird* menacingly circled the hospital, squawking. We never got it back in its cage again. It would disappear and reappear in various places. I would discover it brooding over my home. Other times I would hear it had been looming over one of the other family members home, until the day it became ours.

It was Thanksgiving Day when *the despicable bird* became ours.

We didn't want it any more than my mother-in-law had. Again, it didn't care. It knew she no longer recognized it, so it no longer had the power to torment her. Consequently, it attached itself to us, inflicting its pain. We tried to shoo it away, but it refused to leave. It seemed to feed on this response as well as take pleasure in our distress. It was malicious, vexing, and annoying. I thought there must be a way to be rid of *the awful bird*.

It was in February I was given the way to be free of the tormenting misery of *the bird*. The freedom happened in a moment as I heard it in my heart: *A Bird Named Payn.*

A name. The Spirit of Grace gave *the bird* a name—Payn.

Such a simple act, but powerful. Like a ginormous monster instantly shrinking down to the size of a canary no longer needing a cage. *The bird* with a name belonged there. Its name defined it, gave it boundaries, and removed its power to wreak the havoc it once did so well. Before it was bound by a name, it existed in the darkness of threatening fear, changing in appearance and definition. The complex ambiguity is what gave it such great power to inflict pain.

Ann has been battling Alzheimer's for several years. It's called by some *The Long Goodbye*. It's an agonizing, erratic, devastatingly pain-filled journey. Encountering the unknown and vague are all too common on this journey. Anxiety and fear visit frequently. *Payn* fed on the kaleidoscope of fears and uncertainties. Fear is an insatiable monster seeking to destroy. *Payn* was hers as she walked through losing her memory and knowledge of self. Once she progressed past knowing her condition, then *Payn* became ours.

Emotions need to be put somewhere. Silently caging them without validation, they simply escape again. When they sit in our soul unnamed and/or ineffectively tended to, they rot and fester. The numerous emotions we feel as we watch Ann walk out the end of her life, not knowing who she is—or be able to care for herself at all—can be summed up into *Payn.*

As I left the facility, after feeding Ann her lunch that day, *Payn* sat quietly on my shoulder. I felt *Payn* sitting there, but I had peace. I was happy to comfort and care for one who comforted and cared for me when I needed it. The fears have been properly silenced with love. The fears shrieking and squawking *"am I doing enough?"; "have I done the right things?"; "what do I do now?"; "what will I do when she's gone?"; "what if there's something I could do, but I don't know what it is?"; "I've prayed for her, and she didn't get better where did I fail?"*; and so on, were silenced by the Spirit of Grace. He comforted me in that what I'm doing, I'm doing in love with all my heart, and it's enough. I felt the Spirit of Grace with me as I walked to my car.

While walking, I received a text from a family member who'd been at lunch with Ann and me. Sorrow filled my heart as I read it. I watched *Payn* lift off my shoulder to torment the sender of the text. They'd encountered the monster of chaotic feelings I'd just tamed, and they didn't know what to do with them. I simply replied, *I understand*. It was painful being unable to define what was going on in their heart for them. I wanted to help, but I understood their emotional turmoil doesn't belong to me. My journey is mine, and theirs uniquely belongs to them. I found *Payn* required identification, acceptance, and comfort. The Spirit of Grace brought me light to see, the power to accept, and the comfort I needed. I know He will for them as well.

Later, I returned to the story of *Payn*. I knew I needed to share it with others dealing with those monstrous emotions. As I prepared it to share, *Payn* attempted to revert into the monster. Once again, I felt those feelings. The ones the unnamed monster of chaotic emotion stirred within me. I reached for the comfort of the Spirit of Grace, stood up, and walked around. *Payn* rose and squawked at me. I called a few friends to ground myself, but none answered. As I did this, I noticed my mother-in-law's phone number still on my phone's favorites list. My heart sank. Tears flowed. She doesn't have her cell phone anymore. *Payn* swooped at me as the opposites collided: Ann being alive, yet so much of her is gone. *Payn* squawked at me again with truth and lies, mixed together. Words taunting me how there was a time I would've called Ann for comfort, but now I couldn't; therefore, I have none, no one. I reminded both *Payn* and myself I'm not alone. I know the Spirit of Grace is with me. Still, I feel, I feel, I feel. I continued looking for a human connection. I finally got in touch with someone. I told them how I needed a minute to talk to someone and told them what was going on. They comforted me. I think we spoke for less than five minutes. But it wasn't about them or my being able or unable to connect to another human. It was about me refusing to believe the lies. The pile of lies taunting me that I was alone, no one understood or cared and that *Payn* was a monster again. It was not the *end of the world* as the monstrous feelings screamed.

I've learned what we perceive to be true becomes our reality. We respond to the perception. Regardless of it being true or not, positive or negative, it's what we believe. Because of this, and whether we like it or not, we operate under the directive of faith—the thing we believe in our heart. It can work for us or against us. I've had it work against me a great deal. Fortunately, on this day, I recognized my need to take control of my perception. What I knew to be true needed to supersede the emotion, telling me a different story. I succeeded. Then I went back into my phone to delete Ann's phone number. *Payn* squawked I would be deleting her (as if her phone number were actually her and as if I held that kind of power). What a lie. I glared at *Payn,* and it shut up. Ann's contact information still had her old address. The one prior to the memory care facility, as well as the landline phone from prior to that—the phone number she had with her husband, my father-in-law before he passed away. More memories, more feelings. I chose to cherish the memories and called *Payn* by name. Validating my emotions, I embraced *Payn*. I had every right to feel my sorrow. It was mine. Authentic love is what projected the deep sorrow. Then I deleted the contact that no longer existed and sat in gentle silence, paying the price for love.

Grief is the last act of love we can give to those we loved. Where there is deep grief there was great love.

—Unknown

KEY POINTS

- Physical, mental, and emotional pain are all different, yet all need tending to. All need comfort, care, and healing.
- Unresolved mental and emotional pain leak into our lives, creating a mess. To fully own the mess, we need to own the pain that accompanies it.
- Sharing with others helps us heal because healing happens together.
- When we ask God for help, He embraces and comforts us because He's the Spirit of Grace.
- Stress is part of life, and there are different kinds. Therefore, it's to our benefit to learn how to handle it in healthy ways.
- Complex emotional pain can be tamed by the Spirit of Grace.

YOU CAN ASK GOD FOR HELP

God help me deal with the pain in my life. Comfort me and heal me. If I need to build a strategy, please show me how. If I need to name something, please show me what. Help me embrace what's rightfully mine and use it to move forward.

NOTES

How Nancy Took Ownership Of Her Life

We just have to be who we are and be okay with that. Because truly, who we are is enough.

—Nancy Bouwens

Nancy and I are fellow Tribe Writers. We met in 2017 at an organized meet up before the Tribe Conference in Franklin, Tennessee. Nancy is a real sweetheart with a smile that lights up a room. She's also a strong and courageous woman who's been through the fire in the last few years. When I asked to interview her, I was aware of how she took ownership of her battle with cancer, but there was so much more.

A string of traumas invaded Nancy's life-threatening to kill each of her children, one at a time. In 2011 she had one son in college, another son who lived in town and a daughter living across the country who was married with kids. In October, one son was in a terrible car accident, landing him in the hospital. After the new year, her other son was diagnosed with Guillain-Barre Syndrome and was in the hospital. In May 2012, her daughter, who was fourteen weeks pregnant, suffered a massive stroke, landing her in the hospital. All this happened within a seven-month period.

But long before all that, emotional trauma had already driven Nancy to her knees. The son who lived in town was making poor choices, breaking her heart, and she took ownership of her pain with prayer. *"If I was going to wear out my knees, it was going to be praying for that kid."* It was one of those poor choices that led to the accident, leaving him with two fractured vertebrae and a broken leg. But thankfully, alive. A situation like that creates confusing emotions. In my interview with Nancy, she pointed to the grace of God repeatedly.

Nancy's prayers were not in vain. Change didn't happen overnight because we're free moral agents, and prayer isn't magic. For ten long years, she prayed. It was painful to watch her son suffer the consequences of his choices. And then came the tragic loss of his first child—a horrible loss for Nancy as well. But then Nancy beamed with pride as told me how he is now. *"He's a father, a husband, a successful business owner (as a licensed journeyman electrician). He's just amazing, and I'm proud of who he has become and what he's overcome to do that."* She never gave up on him. Tempted by the reeling emotions, but her will was steadfast. *"If it meant dragging him out of bed almost physically, sometimes to get him to school . . . I drove him to his electrician certification state test . . . I just kept speaking life into him."* And that is what Nancy is all about—the power of our words breathing life into others.

Nancy began coaching women in 2012. Here is a person going through events that would wipe out some people emotionally, and she reached inside herself, owned her pain, and used it to help others. *"I believe that we have the power to change the world with our words. The Bible says that there's life and death in the power of our tongue. And I think that we can bring life, into someone's world by encouragement, by speaking life, and we can also kill them emotionally and spiritually by the words that we say."* As Nancy was praying for her son, she prayed for her other two children as well. She spoke life over all of them.

Her son that was diagnosed with Guillain-Barre Syndrome was in the hospital for weeks. They didn't know if he'd ever walk again, but he did. *"It was a long recovery . . . but after regaining his strength he was moving very slowly, but able to go back to col-*

lege, and even study abroad the following semester." Years later he's serving in the Peace Corps overseas.

And Nancy's daughter? At twenty-nine-years old and with five kids, she fought her way back to health. Nancy lamented she couldn't be there physically to help much, but she did what she could, and she prayed. It took four years for her daughter to get back on her feet, but she did. *"She's my inspiration. She has fought hard. She is a story that doesn't quit. She is my little warrior. Her family and her husband have supported and loved on her. And it's a whole book in and of itself."*

So, the three tragedies were grueling, but have a happy ending. But trauma wasn't done invading Nancy's life. In 2018 on the sixteenth of March, she heard words no one ever wants to hear—you have cancer. Breast cancer, Right Invasive Carcinoma grade 3. *"I just remember laying my head down on the desk, as I heard the words, you have cancer. I thought, Oh, sweet Jesus."* She sat for a minute. Paused. Then she took ownership once again. *"Okay, Jesus, we're going to do this. And if we're going to do it, I want to give you glory. And I want people to see you in every step that I take. You're going to have to help me. I don't wanna take a breath without you."* Thirteen months later, she had a clear mammogram.

This woman's strength and faith are extraordinary. In the interview, we talked about where she got her strength. Her faith, of course. But Nancy drew strength from other sources as well. For example, her parents. When I asked her if she had any childhood trauma, she said no. Her growing up years were steady and stable. As she expounded on it, I was surprised. She had parents somewhat similar to me—*"German, dig your heels in and work hard. You know, don't be emotional and don't say a whole lot."* But contrary to my experience with that temperament growing up, she knew she was loved. Somehow, someway her parents conveyed to her that she was loved. Even though Nancy doesn't remember displays of affection, she has no doubt of their love. She says they just have trouble expressing it. *"My folks were steady, strong, and solid. And even if they didn't tell me I was wonderful, and I love you, and I believe in you and all that. So many kids don't have that. That's a legacy they're leaving us. Without that, we wouldn't have made it through what we did. So as a couple, that quiet, strong strength I saw in my parents, I know, I can be that for my children, in spite of all of these things."*

Before he died, Nancy received a precious gift of validating words from her dad on a family vacation to Disney World. *"We were taking the boat back from the main park back to Disney World. And my dad looked at me, he said, 'You're a good mom.' I took a picture of him right after that. I don't ever want to forget what that felt like to hear him say that because normally he wouldn't."* Words of life to be cherished forever. Many people go their entire life, never hearing words like that from their parents.

Nancy's experience reminds me of a book I read when I was raising my kids. It had multiple contributors sharing stories of things their parents did right. I desperately wanted to raise my kids different than I had been, but I didn't know how. This book comforted me with the truth that no parent does everything right, but every parent can do something right. Nancy's parents did something right. They modeled quiet inner strength that carried her through difficult times.

During Nancy's battle with cancer, she was surrounded with words of life by countless friends. Both in person and online. One of the first things she did when she got the news of cancer was start a Facebook group "Nancy's Unstoppable Journey Through Breast Cancer." She knew how important community would be and reached for help. Help showed up through prayer, letters, cards, meals, hugs, rides to and from appointments, people who would *"sit with me while I puked my guts out. People who shaved my head when my hair was falling out."* Her gratitude for how people loved on her in practical ways brings her to tears. *"Just the other day, I opened my box of cards of people who had sent things. I didn't even . . . I didn't even touch them. I just opened it. Even now, just talking about it. I just want to weep with gratitude, because I don't know how people go through stuff like that without their people."* Being surrounded by so much love and support provided additional strength for Nancy.

Knowing we're loved and that we matter is so important. Many people struggle with their value, including Nancy. She told me how it's been a constant struggle her whole life. The question 'who do you think you are?' constantly attacks her value. *"It's a constant choosing to believe who I am, I've been created in the image of God, I'm a daughter of the Most High God. I've been called with a purpose. I have to keep telling myself those things all the time."*

Words. Nancy believes in the power of words. She sees all the hurt, pain, and trauma in the world and is compelled to make a difference. She does it with words—when coaching, and in everyday life. At the grocery store, for example, Nancy makes it a point to see the cashier. Not just see as in eye vision but see them as a person. She does this by genuinely ask how their day is going. *"Sometimes you get tears running down their face because somebody actually saw them. People aren't seen often enough."*

Technology has caused a divide between people. Automation and the internet have reduced our person to person and face to face relationships. This frustrates Nancy immensely. She knows how much we need human connection. It's what she offers with her coaching. Nancy helps women to see and discover their value and identity. *"Kind of like a treasure hunt, who they are, who they are in Christ, who they are as a woman. And not just who they are, but who they can become, how they can grow. It just blesses me be-*

yond comprehension. I get so much joy out of walking alongside of another woman who's just sick of the status quo, and ready to make a change."

Find out more about Nancy and what he has to offer in the endnotes.

CHAPTER 8

Owning Your Emotions

If your emotional abilities aren't in hand, if you don't have self-awareness, if you are not able to manage your distressing emotions, if you can't have empathy and have effective relationships, then no matter how smart you are, you are not going to get very far.

—Daniel Goleman

HOW TO BEGIN

Emotions. People tend to stuff them, deny them, make excuses for them, or diminish them. None of these are healthy. When our emotions *speak*, we need to listen, because they're trying to tell us something. Listening is just the first part. Owning our emotions takes skill, and a wise person will develop this skill. I'm working on it. The Spirit of Grace is helping me.

I dare you to own your emotions, and the skillset to maximize their benefits.

OWN YOUR FEELINGS BECAUSE THEY'RE VALID

Don't let anyone invalidate or minimize how you feel. If you feel something, you feel it and it's real to you. Nothing anyone says has the power to invalidate that ever. No one else lives in your body. No one else sees life through your eyes. No one else has lived through your experiences. And so, no one else has the right to dictate or judge how you feel. Your feelings are important and you deserve to be heard. They are inherently valid and they matter. Don't let anyone make you believe otherwise.

—Unknown

I write about feelings (or emotions) often. They come under attack, causing people to suffer. I'm here to defend them because they're an important part of who we are, and we need them. People stuff them, explain them away, negate them, deride them, and qualify them for various reasons. Others consider emotions sinful. For example, I came across a person who claimed God didn't create people with emotions. They said emotions were the result of the fall of mankind. This person was vicious in their words while claiming to be walking in love as a follower of Jesus. That's ridiculous. There was no love coming from this person. It's that kind of twisted information that messes up people's minds. I suffered from twisted information that said what I felt didn't matter. It was a lie. My feelings do matter, so do yours. In fact, they're essential.

Emotions are indicators. You feel something for a reason. Emotions have a valid purpose, a valid reason, a valid function. Feelings need to be validated. We do this by owning them.

Sounds simple, but for those learning this as an adult, it's quite difficult. I celebrate the parents teaching their children about emotions instead of squashing them. Squashing them brings harm.

The reason feelings are valid is they're telling you something. They have a point to make, and you need to listen to them so you can respond optimally. Sometimes they're hard to identify if you're emotionally illiterate like I was. I'm still learning. Sometimes there's a mix of them, which makes it more difficult. They need to be unraveled and made sense of. It takes courage to own your feelings. There'll be the supporters, and there'll be the aggressors. The better we get at owning them, the stronger we stand against the aggressors who try to steal a part of who we are. By owning our emotions, we're empowered to process them. If we fail to do this, our emotions will *process* us, and the result isn't pretty.

Owning your emotions validates a part of who God made you to be.

OWN YOUR INNER LIFE: IT DIRECTS WHO YOU BECOME

Until you make the unconscious conscious, it will direct your life and you will call it fate.

—C.G. Jung

My messy meltdown that *seemed* to come out of nowhere in *Owning Your Pain* had been building silently for years. Little did I know this epic meltdown would be a major pivot point in my life.

It not only revealed my lack of skills to cope with life in general but specifically with my emotions. I'd learned so much, and come so far, but this event was a rude awakening. I questioned myself. *Had I learned anything? Had I really grown? How could this happen? Who am I?*

The meltdown stirred up these questions about my inner life. I had a choice to make. I could ignore what happened and continue with the status quo knowing it most likely would happen again, or I could take ownership of what was going on in my inner life, and therefore of who I wanted to be.

I wanted to be stronger than my circumstances. I wanted to be stronger than the pressures of life. I wanted to be a better person. To do this, I had to take ownership of my inner life because it's where our life flows out of. The Bible says in Proverbs 4:23, "Keep your heart with all vigilance, for from it flow the springs of life." This makes our inner life of vast importance.

What's going on in your inner life is who you are.

OWN THE VALUE OF EMOTIONS AND THEIR USEFULNESS

Our feelings are not there to be cast out or conquered. They're there to be engaged and expressed with imagination and intelligence.

—T.K. Coleman

My Friend, Validation, taught me feelings are vital. She came to help me after the messy meltdown in my new journey to understand and deal with feelings in a more productive way. I first met her while I was in counseling for the writing of my first book. I'll call it my *"journey to emerge."* I found her priceless. Back then, she gave me the power to tame the monster named Trauma. Before I met her, I'd struggled to learn and grow emotionally for years. Although the effort wasn't wasted due to the progress I *did* make; it just wasn't enough. I'd read books, listened to self-help gurus, teachers and preachers, and they helped, but none of them had introduced me to Val. I needed her, and here she was again.

So many voices in the world look down on the emotional landscape of humans. Some talk about emotions as if they are our enemy and need to be eliminated, calling them dangerous. Others see them as petty, unpredictable, and/or unreliable, so believe they need to be disregarded. I used to wrestle with these views before I met Val. She showed me these attitudes are defective and destructive. Validation drew a different picture of emotions for me. One thing she told me is our feelings are unique to us. They're a part of who we are—what makes us, Us. I had trouble accepting this because my view had always been; they were separate from me. How else would I be able to eliminate or disregard them? That would mean I was trying to eliminate or disregard a part of who I am.

Wait!

That's exactly what I once tried to do until *The Pursuer* intervened; but that story is in my first book. On this new journey, Validation called emotions valuable and useful. Val said skill is what's needed to properly utilize emotions. Skill. I liked that word. It made me think of sword fighting. She compared it to the skill needed to pilot a plane.

We can become skilled in utilizing our emotions by owning them.

OWN EMOTIONAL SKILLS: IT'S LIKE BEING AN AIRLINE PILOT

If we lack emotional intelligence, whenever stress rises the human brain switches to autopilot and has an inherent tendency to do more of the same, only harder. Which, more often than not, is precisely the wrong approach in today's world.

—Robert K. Cooper

When we board an airplane, we exert a certain amount of trust. Whether we're aware of it or not we're placing our lives in the hands of another person. This person sits behind the controls of this massive machine that by all appearances, should never be able to get off of the ground. Why do we do this? Because we have places to go. Why do we trust? Because we believe the pilots know what they're doing. They have skill. They know things we don't, like the law of lift and thrust, how to deal with turbulence, what turbulence is for that matter, and much more.

Even though I've had it explained to me how lift and thrust work, I still marvel at the seeming magicalness going on when the airplane lifts off of the ground. Magicalness? Yes, it's a word, I looked it up, and it's an appropriate one. This thing that's contrary to our perceptions of being possible is happening, and it feels magical like there should be glitter and unicorns. It's breathtaking to me. Although I understand the rational information of how it's happening, when I *see nothing* holding the plane up, I sit captivated for a while until I start to feel normal again. *Normal*, as if floating up in the clouds is a natural, effortless, everyday thing anyone could do. Our minds are strange like that. We rationalize things we don't understand.

We travel on our emotions in similar ways that planes fly. The word travel indicates we're going somewhere. Both airplanes and emotions are powerful modes of transportation. Traveling by plane is fairly simple. We purchase an airline ticket and fly to our destination—unless there's trouble. Our emotions aren't always that cut and dried. It's possible we're unaware of what we're feeling, or we may not realize we're going anywhere. We may think we're *just* feeling. But those feelings are going to take us somewhere because we're going to do something with them. We will act, react, or refuse to act. If we haven't made a conscious decision of where we want to go with the feeling we're experiencing, we may *find* ourselves somewhere we don't want to be. Like in my epic meltdown, my emotions went on autopilot.

Some of the things emotions move us to do are: make a decision, choose a career, have an argument, act out, compulsive behaviors, self-medication, and the list goes on. Another similarity is this: both planes and emotions utilize the unseen to maneuver. Air is invisible and is the force that pushes a plane up or down. Emotions are also not visible to our eyeballs. They're the unseen forces that lift us with positive feelings like pleasure or push us down with negative ones like sorrow, or anger.

Pilots know how critical it is to understand how the air can move a plane up, or an air pocket can cause it to drop dramatically. It's even more important to understand how to respond to our emotions because they are closer to us than the air surrounding a plane. If the skill needed is not employed, both can *crash & burn* as the saying goes. Neither are pretty.

How you pilot your emotions will determine where and how you land.

OWN LESSONS FROM WEATHER TO HELP YOU PILOT BETTER

Emotional intelligence is the ability to sense, understand, and effectively apply the power and acumen of emotions as a source of human energy, information, connection, and influence.

—Robert K. Cooper, PhD

Weather happens. There are places it's easier to predict than others. Ask a meteorologist. They understand. Nevertheless, they still attempt to predict what the weather will do when it seems difficult or impossible. It's a wise pilot who factors the weather into their flight plan.

We feel. Our feelings resemble the weather in that they're only predictable at times. Unlike a meteorologist who only has the exterior weather to study, we have emotional weather both within, as well as around us. This requires great skill. If it takes the meteorologist to predict and the pilot to respond, it means two people are working on one outcome. We, being a single entity, have the job of directing our lives, weaving together both the external weather (circumstances that happen around us) as well as the internal weather (states of anxiety, grief, depression, anger, guilt, worthlessness, shame, etc.). That's a tall order for an individual to address. If we listen to the voices saying to ignore our feelings, it can be compared to asking a pilot to ignore tornados, hurricanes, or lightning storms.

Our internal weather of feelings can be much more dangerous than the environmental weather around a plane. Emotions, passions, reactions, hormones, chemical imbalances, etc., are capable of wielding greater intensities of chaotic pressure than tornados or hurricanes, as well as higher surges of electricity than lightning storms.

Pilots can choose to fly around dangerous stormy weather, as well they should. We don't have that luxury. It's not possible for us to fly around our inner storms. They're inside of us, a part of us. We'll respond either intentionally or passively. Validation taught me it's not wise to ignore (be passive), disregard (invalidate), or downplay emotions.

Failing to own our emotional weather can have disastrous results.

OWN YOUR EMOTIONS AS GIFTS FROM GOD

So how do I come to the conclusion that emotions are a gift and that they are good? All of them . . . First, God made humans in His image; Secondly, God reveals who He is in the Bible and He reveals Himself as an emotional being.

—Tami Schow

By now I'm sure you understand I'm saying our emotions are a big deal. So, am I suggesting we should be focused on ourselves and how we feel all the time? Absolutely not. We have a life to live! Airplane pilots go to school to learn how to master the complicated machines. But they don't live at school.

Learning and becoming skilled regarding emotions will bring about a more rewarding life and help us to relate better with others. So where are we to *"go to school?"* Because we're created in the image of God who is both relational and emotional, I think He's the best teacher. Using the word emotional as a positive description of God wasn't easy for me at first. My perception of the word emotional had been negative. My life was full of *"you're too emotional"* and *"stop being so emotional"* as if emotions were bad. I was expected to just shut them off with a switch. For a season, I tried. It took my *"journey to emerge"* for that to change.

We're emotional creatures—all of us. There's no shame in that. God feels joy, sorrow, pleasure, and anger, to name a few. When we experience emotions, we're being like Him. Our emotions aren't just valid. They're a gift from God. We need to unwrap them and learn how God designed them to be utilized and enjoyed.

Owning your emotions as gifts will help you learn how to use them.

OWN YOUR EMOTIONS AS SOPHISTICATED INTERNAL WEATHER

He has made everything beautiful in its time. He has also set eternity in the human heart; yet no one can fathom what God has done from beginning to end.

—Solomon

Emotions and the weather. Who'd think they would have anything to do with each other? I certainly didn't. But they do.

Weather. What comes to your mind when you hear that word? Maybe you think of a sunny day, or perhaps a storm. Maybe your mind goes to small talk because people say the weather is always a safe topic of conversation.

I didn't think much of the weather. It was just there. I didn't know a lot about it other than the obvious things. I thought it was weird for people to care so much about it, watching it on television all the time. I would get the weather forecast and call it a day. I live in Michigan, where unpredictable weather is the norm. We have a saying here: *If you don't like the weather stick around because it'll change.* I imagine that fed into my lack of reliance on it. I didn't trust it. But I've learned some things. Weather is more than sunny or rainy. In fact, it's quite intricate in how it works. We simplify it because we usually don't need to know all those complex details. Yet, they're there. To oversimplify, the weather is the condition of the atmosphere. What is the atmosphere? It's the air surrounding the earth. What is meant by *condition*? It's what's going on in the air, much of which we can't see. There are things affecting the condition of the atmosphere. These things are terms used when talking about the weather—wind, visibility, precipitation, temperature, humidity, pressure, clouds, and sunshine. Eight things! There are eight factors employed to determine the weather.

Now, I think watching the weather is intriguing. I have respect for its complexity.

Emotion. What does that word bring to your mind? Is it a simple answer or complicated? For me, it's much more complicated than what I've learned about the weather; but, we can learn from their commonalities.

Both emotions and weather are a condition of an atmosphere. The atmosphere in the weather is the air around us; whereas, with emotion, it's the *air* inside of us, also known as spirit. I'm sure you've heard someone referring to the air or *atmosphere* of a place being happy or tense or strange. That's the *spirit* in the *air* streaming from people's internal atmospheres.

How many emotions do we have to deal with in our internal atmosphere? My research found the answer inconclusive with a range from four[15] to thirty-four thousand.[16] I repeat – four to thirty-four thousand! As I researched more, I found a place that said we have an infinite[17] amount of emotions. How in the world are we supposed to deal with them? Many of us don't. We let them deal with us. I used to live like that. I had no understanding there were skills available.

Validate the sophistication of your internal weather and the need for skill.

OWN THE CLIMATE OF YOUR SOUL

As water reflects the face, so one's life reflects the heart.
—Solomon

Where you live on the planet affects how dependable a forecast might be. When I lived in Arizona for a few years, I saw this first hand. Unlike Michigan, the forecasts in Arizona are more accurate. I learned this the hard way.

One morning I left all the windows wide open in my house, disregarding the forecast predicting rain. Bad choice. As predicted, there was a downpour, and I came home from work to a mess in every room I needed to clean up.

Lesson? Learning the climate where you live changes everything. Some places are known for certain kinds of storms, or the lack of them. It's always good to be warned of a coming storm. Information is our friend here. This friend can help us to prepare.

Our souls have a climate as well. This *climate* consists of our mind, spirit, and emotions. It's where we *live* or how we deal with things. The emotional aspect of our soul climate is made up by our temperament, moods, attitudes, and mindsets. They affect how we handle life. Who we are and what we have been through is what forms this *climate*. The mental aspect of our soul climate is made up of mindsets, perceptions, and filters. We'll talk more about this in the chapter on *Owning Your Mind*.

As it's helpful to learn the weather climate. It's also helpful to learn our soul climate. Our soul climate shows us where we live, and we can decide if we like it. If you don't like the weather climate of where you live, you can move to another climate. Likewise, it's true of our souls. We can *move* by growing and changing on the inside. Due to the climate, I found in my soul, I *moved* many times by taking ownership and growing. I still don't *live* where I'd like to, but it's much nicer than where I started.

Owning the climate of your soul will help you handle life better.

OWN THE POWER OF INFORMATION AND PREPARATION

... everyone who hears these words of mine and puts them into practice is like a wise man who built his house on the rock. The rain came down, the streams rose, and the winds blew and beat against that house; yet it did not fall, because it had its foundation on the rock. But everyone who hears these words of mine and does not put them into practice is like a foolish man who built his house on sand. The rain came down, the streams rose, and the winds blew and beat against that house, and it fell with a great crash.

—Jesus

Every day is not always sunny or happy. Sometimes, it rains. Sometimes, it storms. Sometimes, disasters and tragedy strike around us or inside us. How are we to deal with all this? Prepare as much as possible. To prepare, we need to listen to the information we have available. For example, if I would've heeded the forecast predicting rain and closed my windows, I wouldn't have had anxiety while I was at work, or the mess to clean up when I got home. Instead, I would've had a sense of peace and relief knowing I'd closed the windows and the rain wouldn't affect me. I didn't listen, and so I suffered.

When there are weather reports warning us of hurricanes, tornados, and the like, it's wise to take the appropriate steps to prepare in relation to where you live—your climate. Do you need to board up windows? Do you need to go buy water and food? Do you need sandbags because you live near the water? Do you need to leave the area? Other questions vary due to the severity of what is expected, and the climate/location of where you live.

Likewise, in our inner climate; this is where we store our attitude and beliefs. The greater the amount of preparation we have, the better. The more prepared we feel, the less anxiety we'll have because preparation provides confidence that lessens fear.

Life has forecasts too. There are things in life we can emotionally prepare for because we know they're coming. Starting a new job, having a baby, kids going away to school, teenage years, moving, and retirement are a few examples. Do you have the information you need? Is there a book you can read, a class you can take, or a person you could talk with? Do you know what you need, or do you need to do some research? Do you want God to help you?

Utilizing the information available helps us prepare for emotional weather.

OWN HOW YOU EMOTIONALLY MANEUVER

We define emotional intelligence as the subset of social intelligence that involves the ability to monitor one's own and others' feelings and emotions, to discriminate among them and to use this information to guide one's thinking and actions.

—Salovey and Mayer

We can learn a lot from airplanes and helicopters. Storms affect their ability to fly in numerous ways: the type of storm, as well as how they fly.

Large airplanes can handle a lot of different kinds of weather. They can maneuver well in storms. Some people are like that. They can naturally handle more. They have a strong and stable inner climate due to resilience and emotional intelligence. Things don't bother them much. They're able to deal with what comes at them and then move on.

Small airplanes shouldn't be airborne in a thunderstorm.[18] There's nothing wrong with small planes. It's just what they are. They're not able to handle what the larger plane can. They have different maneuvering skills. What can we learn here? How you're able to maneuver will determine how well you can fly in rough weather. We can know we're a *light-weight* in our climate if our soul is wounded, things tend to bother us, we tend to fly off the handle or have a hard time letting things go. If this is true of us, then it's wise to avoid or get out of emotionally difficult situations. If it's not possible, then we need to ask for help from someone stronger so we can *land safely*.

Helicopters[19] fly differently than planes and aren't as stable. Like the smaller plane, it doesn't make them bad; it's just how they function. There are situations they don't handle well. The situation is the problem, not the helicopter. Likewise, with people, there are situations we can't handle well. It's the situation that's the problem, not the person. Knowing how we handle things, how we maneuver emotionally is essential information so we can avoid harmful situations or get the assistance we need.

Pretending we're something we're not, could end in disaster.

OWN HOW THE POWER AND DANGER OF WIND APPLIES TO YOU

Peter got down out of the boat, walked on the water and came toward Jesus. But when he saw the wind, he was afraid and, beginning to sink, cried out, "Lord, save me!" Immediately Jesus reached out his hand and caught him.

—Matthew

Due to the laws that govern flight, wind[20] has a greater effect on airplanes than rain. Lift and thrust are key laws that deal with air, but the wind is air in motion. Wind can be quite dangerous. Sudden changes in the wind can force an aircraft up, down, sideways, and even affect its speed. This is called wind shear.[21]

Wind in nature can be compared to sudden trauma in our lives. In flight and in life, without the necessary skills, the results are catastrophic. This is the reason some planes overshoot a runway and crash. Sudden trauma in our lives, if we're unable to maneuver, cause an inner crash. But wind can also work for us.[22] When airplanes encounter tailwinds and jet streams, they can make a trip take much less time. Likewise, when we're in a season of our lives full of joy or enthusiasm, time seems to fly, and we soar in our soul. When we encounter the wind (or anointing) of the Spirit of Grace, we're empowered in supernatural ways: the disciples of Jesus on the day of Pentecost, for example. The strength of the tailwind for the plane, the euphoria of our positive emotions, or the intensity of the anointing we encounter, dictate the extent of the forward progress.

Winds don't only come from the front (headwind) or the back (tailwind) they can also come from the side—crosswind[23]. All these directions of wind effect the airplane by speeding it up, slowing it down or turbulence, which is uncomfortable. Likewise, circumstances in our lives can create winds: tailwind (joy, praise, favor), headwind (opposition, strife), or crosswind (uncertainty, trauma).

High gusting winds for a helicopter[24] can be catastrophic at takeoff as it crashes with itself—the rotor blades with the tail boom. Turbulence has the ability to toss helicopters hundreds of feet up or down in seconds. Compare this to a sudden *wind* of trouble for a person. The sudden rush of emotions can collide internally and cause an internal crash, where a person might turn the sudden emotions they feel against themselves. I have done both. In either case, when a person crashes into themselves via emotional turbulence or self-attacking, they need help, and they may not have the presence of mind to ask for it.

When the wind is working for you, enjoy it and help others; and when it's contrary, cry out for the help you need.

OWN HELP WHEN EMOTIONALLY BLINDSIDED

Suddenly a furious storm came up on the lake, so that the waves swept over the boat. But Jesus was sleeping. The disciples went and woke him, saying, "Lord, save us! We're going to drown!" He replied, "You of little faith, why are you so afraid?" Then he got up and rebuked the winds and the waves, and it was completely calm. The men were amazed and asked, "What kind of man is this? Even the winds and the waves obey him!"

—Matthew

In the weather, we usually have a warning for a storm. For example, *tornado watches* or *conditions are favorable* for something to happen. These give us the opportunity to prepare. But in our lives, it's not always the case. There are plenty of awful things that occur we never saw coming. Tragedies, accidents, deaths, terrorism, and the list goes on. They sucker punch us in our emotions. They cause trauma to our soul, and we reel from the pain. We find ourselves asking why. *Why did God let this happen?* What are we to do in these times when we can't see straight due to the pain and anguish in our souls? What are we to do when our souls silently scream for reasons, for clarity, a way to make sense of this awfulness?

I use these three things:

1. Reach inside for whatever preparation I have in my soul. Words, songs, lessons.
2. Reach out for someone to help. Call someone or show up at their house or workplace. Ask for prayer and guidance.
3. Take the advice of Mother Teresa—trust God. A man came to her, wanting her to pray for him. He asked her to pray for clarity for him. She said no. He was stunned and asked

why not, saying he thought she had clarity, and he wanted it. She told him, *"I have never had clarity; what I have always had was trust."* She prayed for him to trust God.

Reach in, reach out, and grab ahold of trust. These three things can carry you through anything.

Take all the help God provides because the wind still obeys Him.

OWN WHAT YOU HAVE WHEN THE TRAUMA STRIKES

Let us hold unswervingly to the hope we profess, for he who promised is faithful.

—Paul

Reach in, reach out, and grab ahold of trust. I did these three things on the day my heart broke into a million pieces by an unexpected phone call. My son called to disconnect from our family, to say *I love you* and *good-bye*.

Reaching in, I found these words in my heart, *I have a blood-bought right to enjoy my children,* and as if on autopilot, they escaped my lips. They were the fruit of preparation I didn't know I needed from two verses in the Bible I'd memorized and prayed over my children for years.

Reaching out, I called a minister friend crying in pain and asking for her to pray in agreement with the words I'd found in my heart. She prayed and encouraged me.

Grabbing ahold of trust, I handed my traumatized soul to the only one who was able to do anything, the Spirit of Grace. All my questions. All my pain. I chose to trust God through the trauma, and the long journey of faith full of grief and pain.

By trusting God in the pain, He provided me with continuous help. Others came alongside me with practical help and encouragement as the days went on.

I've deeply related to the story of the Shunamite woman in the Bible many times over the years, this time included. We had a *little room on the roof, with a chair and a table* for ministers to stay at our house when they were in town, like the Shunamite. We called ours the missionary room. I was given a son by the power of God when I was told I was barren like the Shunamite was. Having a son wasn't her idea. Having my son was God's idea. Trauma struck the Shunamite. Trauma struck me. Her son suddenly died, and she responded with an audacious resolution—he would live. She hadn't asked for this child, and she held Elisha responsible.

Like the Shunamite, I lost my son with a phone call. He wasn't dead physically, but had chosen to detach from the family. As I hung up the phone, and my heart left my chest, the audacious cry of the Shunamite rose in me to the one who gave me my son. I held God responsible. The Shunamite rode to Elisha's place with her dead son and returned home with him alive. I carried my estranged son to the Lord God. It wasn't as quick as the Shunamite, but I have returned with my son, alive to me and fully restored. Great is the Lord. He is faithful.

When trauma arose, it was a disastrous thunderstorm. The Shunamite saw the rainbow. I chose to see the same rainbow through my tears.

Suffering trauma is an emotional storm God has a rainbow for.

KEY POINTS

- The reason feelings are valid is they're telling you something.
- Owning your emotions validates a part of who God made you to be.
- What's going on in your inner life is who you are.
- We travel on our emotions in a similar way planes fly.
- Owning your emotions as gifts will help you learn how to use them.
- Utilizing the information available helps us prepare for emotional weather.
- Pretending we're something we're not, could end in disaster.
- Reach in, reach out, and grab ahold of trust.
- Suffering trauma is an emotional storm God has a rainbow for.

YOU CAN ASK GOD FOR HELP

Dear God, help me to see my emotions as a gift and enjoy them. Help me develop the skills I need to utilize them. Help me reach out and not hide when things are rough, and be there for others in their storms. Thank you that the wind still listens to you.

NOTES

How Andre Took Ownership Of His Life

When I really gained my value, it was the most beautiful thing ever. Because I realized that at the end of the day, I am in control of how I feel. I am in control what shows up in my life. I am in control of how I don't want to feel etc.

—Andre Mills

I met Andre in an unusual way. A woman in a Facebook group I was in asked if anyone was interested in a writing project he was working on. I didn't know Andre or this lady, but I was interested in the project, so I applied. I received a nice professional reply, and a phone interview was set up.

Andre called me, and we talked about his project and what he was looking for. Confident I could deliver, Andre gave me the details of what I was to do. We worked together until my part was completed. He was so professional I had no idea he was only twenty years old. Since then, I've been impressed with Andre's continued growth and love for people.

I asked to interview Andre because I knew he'd taken ownership of his life after a life-altering injury. But in the interview, I got so much more.

Growing up Andre dealt with many bullies. You would never know it now, but Andre had speech problems as a child. *"When I was about five or six years of age, no one could understand me linguistically. Whenever I would speak, no one understood a word that came out of my mouth."* This brought on bullying with people making fun of how he talked. Going to speech therapy and special education classes only worsened the problem. The kids would *"make fun of the fact that I had to get pulled out of class and go to these special classes to assist me with my academic curriculums."* This went on for years until Andre could stand it no more. In the fifth grade, he begged his mom to stop the special classes.

The bullies found a new reason for Andre when he was in middle school. He was the tallest person in his school but *"was terrible at playing basketball."* In addition to being made fun of Andre endured *"a lot of physical abuse at that point, a lot of fights, a lot of altercations."*

The bullies were more violent to Andre in high school. He was no longer terrible at basketball. But that was a problem with the older players. Because he'd become a good player, they were jealous and attacked him physically. It didn't matter if he had a good game or a bad one. They'd throw trash cans on him, cut out the lights in the locker room to get the jump on him and start fights with him in other places. Andre showed me the marks on his arms from being cut and stabbed.

As I listened to Andre talk about these school bullies, it seemed they didn't impact him as deeply as his father. Although he and his father are close now, it wasn't the case growing up. His dad was an ex-marine and former college football star who *"was very aggressive when it came to the things that I was going for in life, such as sports. And he was very demanding that I also had this similar approach on life."* But Andre wasn't aggressive even though he was six feet four inches tall and weighed two hundred pounds. He was more like a teddy bear *"very soft-spoken, soft-hearted."* Andre felt his dad was his biggest bully and was constantly picking on him. He always felt not good enough for him no matter how hard he tried. *"I felt like I was not enough. And so that led to me creating a lot of bad habits, creating a lot of different emotional stresses, a lot of different emotional issues."*

Andre's emotional issues came to a head when he was eighteen years old. He'd gotten so good at basketball it was going to become his career. At seventeen, he was *"labeled an All-American Basketball Player and ranked top 22 in the state of Texas."* In his senior year, he had scholarships and status. His path in life was set to be a professional athlete—until it all came crashing down with an injury.

Andre sustained six fractures in both his legs and was told he'd never play basketball again. Feelings of worthlessness and thoughts of suicide turned into suicide attempts. The inner questions and self-reflection were dizzying. *"If I'm not playing basketball now then who am I? What the heck is this thing called life? Is this really what life is all about?"*

Basketball had become everything, and now it was gone. Andre still struggled academically, and didn't want to go to college. But he felt the peer pressure of *"everyone else"* going. His parents were college graduates. His brother was a high school valedictorian and graduate of A&M. *"What does that make me? Does that make me a bum? Does that make me a loser? What am I then?"*

Andre's high school year became a pivot point where he answered those questions by taking ownership of his life. He realized his life was his to live, and no one else had the right to make his life decisions. Considering the possible ramifications for not going to college, Andre made his choice. *"If I don't want to go, I don't have to go. And it's just that simple."* Making this decision empowered Andre to see life through new eyes, and he felt euphorically reborn. He cast off the victim mentality he had developed and took ownership of accountability. That meant no longer blaming others for what was in life. Andre decided whatever showed up in his life, how he chose to see it, and how he chose to respond was on him alone. Instead of seeing himself impotent and broken, he chose to see himself as whole and complete.

After Andre graduated, he became a voracious learner. Subjects he previously disliked became interesting. Being in control of his choices made all the difference. The self-condemning questions from high school transformed into curiosity. *"Who am I? What am I? Why am I here? And I would always ask myself those questions every single day, why am I here? And what is this life, that life has to offer? And I would always pray that I tap into the right mindset that has me create answers and solutions for my life."* As he sought out the answers for his purpose, he exercised faith in the law of attraction. Soon life coaches and new opportunities showed up. Andre took advantage of them. He signed up for life coaching for a year and then moved to Florida to be mentored. *"When I moved out there is when I really learned the secrets of life. What this life is all about. How to attract my life. What is life. Really going deep into more like a spirituality like practice. Really tapping into who I am and soul searching."*

Andre loves people. He's committed to love and care for humanity. Helping people live a life of freedom, and being who they truly are is his passion. He shared with me when and where this drive to help others began. It was a Saturday morning in June, six months before his injury. A young girl had been kidnapped, raped, and murdered. Discovering this sent Andre *"into this state of empathy"*. For this young girl, for women, for people who have no voice, or feel like they don't matter. He laid on his bed for two hours crying, telling himself he had to do something to impact people's lives. Basketball overshadowed that until his injury derailed his life. *"It was a derailing moment, but it was also a gift at the same time because I never would have pursued, what I've been pursuing these past five, six years, if it had not been for my injury."*

Now Andre runs a personal development research company. Through experiential training, he helps others change their lives. *"We design training seminars for adults, specifically leaders, in-*

fluencers, and anyone who's looking to create a new life for themselves. I teach people how to create a life of inner peace, inner power, and inner passion for their wills, relationships, business, and ultimately, the what's important to people in their lives."

Find out more about Andre and what he has to offer in the endnotes.

CHAPTER 9

Owning Your Mind

Your mind is your instrument. Learn to be its master and not its slave.

—Remez Sasson

HOW TO BEGIN

The mind is a powerful and complex thing. It incorporates more than just the organ called the brain. When we're children, we don't understand this thing called the mind. The things that happen in our minds during our formative years start to play out when we become adults. We develop things called mindsets. This works both for us and against us. Mindsets can be positive or negative and subject to emotional triggers. We form mindsets in every area of our lives. These can help us succeed, as well as destroy our lives. The good news is harmful mindsets can be changed by owning the mind.

I dare you to take possession of every aspect of your mind.

OWN YOUR PERCEPTIONS, THEY MIGHT BE LYING

Perception is reality to the one in the experience.

—Danielle Bernock

You'd think true is true and lies are lies but there's more to it than that. There definitely are absolutes, like the earth is round, gravity, and what God has to say, but what we think of them is what makes the difference. How we think begins with how we perceive. Perhaps that sounds like wordplay, but there's a big difference.

Perception is the way in which we process information. It's a filter. It's part of our mindsets or mental pathways. We encounter situations and endure traumas which affect, or create filters. These filters are how we perceive things. They can distort what's true and turn it into a lie. But the filters can be changed so we can own the truth. For example, I grew up feeling unloved and unwanted. There were various things that created my perception, or filter. After I grew up, I learned my perception was wrong. That meant I grew up believing lies. The lies stole my confidence. Learning we can own our perceptions began with my mom for me. We didn't get along much. I loved her because she was my mom, but I didn't like her, or trust her. One day after I was married with children, she reached out asking me to lunch. I went and she asked if I wanted to be friends. I did. From that day forward, we unveiled the perceptions we had of each other and lies were exposed. It was enlightening. Understanding took their place. We learned we can both see and go through the same things yet filter the circumstances differently, like entering the same room through a different door. The filter causes us to respond differently. We found the truth by owning our own perceptions. Through sharing, we saw our own views were limited, incomplete.

Likewise, your perceptions are yours. They may have truth in them, but they're not the whole story. Others see differently than you because they have their own filters.

Perception is such an intriguing thing. We can be certain in our hearts we know something to be true until we see through someone else's filter. That's part of having a growth mindset (more on that later).

Understanding comes from sharing our differing perceptions. It can be enough simply to consider the other point of view. For example, I wrote an article for Crosswalk.com on *How to Love Your Neighbor as Yourself.* In one of my points, I brought up the story Jesus told about a king. This king had a servant who was deeply in debt to him. When the king called for the servant to settle his account the servant couldn't pay the debt, so the king ordered the servant's property to be sold, and his wife and children taken as slaves. The servant cried out for mercy and more time to pay. The king went beyond. Instead of giving him more time to pay, he forgave the ginormous debt altogether. Afterward, this servant demanded repayment from someone who owed him money but showed no mercy when his debtor cried for it. When the king heard, he was angry and remanded his servant's debt. I'd always thought it meant the debt he'd forgiven was no longer forgiven but put back on his tab. I got a new perspective from a reader who left an intriguing comment. This reader suggested the king didn't reinstate the original debt he'd forgiven, but instead, put a new debt in its place. The reader called it forgiveness failure. I don't know if I agree, but one thing I know: I liked the filter the reader was seeing the king through. It was a filter of integrity because the king followed through with his word of forgiveness for the initial debt, yet exacted justice on the new infraction—lack of mercy and forgiveness.

Owning your perceptions is how to take charge of negative mindsets.

OWN YOUR MINDSET: YOU CAN RISE ABOVE THE NEGATIVE

You cannot have a positive life and a negative mind.

—Joyce Meyer

When we have negative mindsets, they cause condemnation and confusion. Did you ever go through a situation and find yourself somewhere you didn't plan on being: emotionally, mentally or even physically, and you wondered, *how the heck did I get here?* I did many times, and when I asked for help, I was told it's what I'd decided. I wasn't aware of any decisions I'd made. It confused me. Then I'd condemn myself because I felt stupid and saw them as better and smarter than me. It didn't help me change. It made it more painful.

Condemnation and confusion play with the mind. It's not as simple as a thought or two. It's about a thing called mindset.

I discovered mindsets through a book by Joyce Meyer called *The Battlefield of the Mind*. Mindsets are pathways of thought. Pathways take you somewhere. They're how we journey seemingly instantaneously when a situation occurs that might not affect others, but sends us into pervasive fear, confusion, rage or condemnation. When this happens, the situation is called a trigger.

The pathway is the mindset. These pathways or mindsets are built in our childhood by one experience at a time and/or through repetition or succession. Being told over and over you're stupid, suffering the loss of a parent, close family member or friend, witnessing something awful, being bullied, being shamed or humiliated, to name a few. Negative stimuli—single sudden, same repetitive, or multiple various successive—all build negative mindsets.

Overcoming negative mindsets is all about taking charge of them. This is exercising a growth mindset. The first step is to identify what the mindsets are. Start with one. The last time you were triggered. What was the trigger? Write it down. Where did you end up? Write it down. Then you need to identify the pathway your thoughts traveled on—the progression of thoughts. This can be harder to identify. It was for me.

I had many complex negative mindsets. I learned this by disassembling a pathway after suffering a trigger I thought I'd overcome. The surge of emotion was overwhelming, and the people around me were oblivious to what had just happened. Later that day, I set out to deal with this. I wanted this to stop. Surely it can be stopped. I prayed, or maybe complained, to God about how this had to stop, asking Him to help me. He had me sit down and examine what had happened by looking inside my soul for the thoughts and/or feelings as they'd unraveled. I wrote them down, and God showed me how the pathway was created by a lie I was believing. It was a negative mindset that began when I was six years old, from being publicly shamed and humiliated by my first-grade teacher, that hid in the recesses of my soul.

Bringing negative mindsets out into the light empowers us to own them.

OWN A LARGER VIEW: OUR PERSPECTIVES ARE SKEWED

You never really understand a person until you consider things from his point of view... Until you climb inside of his skin and walk around in it.

—Harper Lee

All we know is all we know until we learn more. There's always more to know and learn. It takes a growth mindset to own a larger view. What we know is filtered through our perceptions. It's our perspective. All our perspectives are real to us, but they're skewed because they're incomplete. Knowing this helps us be less opinionated. When we get stuck in our opinion, we fail to understand there's another way to look at things, a larger view. It's called other people's perspectives. There are times when two perspectives seem to clash, yet both are true. This is due to our perception. My mother and I had this problem until we owned a larger view.

Owning a larger view opens you up to healing, growth, and understanding. Bridges can be built in relationships when you own a larger view. My mother and I built a bridge between our misunderstandings that healed our relationship, which caused us both to grow. We did this by enlarging our view to include each other's.

I saw my mother as controlling and insensitive. She saw me as selfish and vain. These things were not true about either of us. In fact, quite the opposite. My mother wanted a better relationship with me and took a courageous step. She set up a meeting for us to talk. It was lunch, and I went because I felt I had to. I had no idea how drastically our lives were about to change. At this lunch meeting, my mom asked me a question that stunned me. *Did I want to be friends?* The thought of friendship with my mother was so outside my thought process, but it was everything this starved-for-parental-affection-soul yearned for, and so I said yes.

Next came the hard work of owning a larger view. By using two primary tools, we learned our skewed perceptions caused us to believe the lies that separated us. The two tools were questions and listening. Many questions followed by active listening. Our questions involved perception; for example, *What were you thinking when you . . .? Why did you do . . .?* Active listening doesn't argue but hears, confirms, and accepts the other person's view *as their truth*. Listening in this way validates the one being heard, which causes understanding, and empathy. Understanding breeds forgiveness.

A primary secret to our success was courage. We took risks. We dared to ask and answer emotionally charged questions. We forced ourselves to be vulnerable to each other. It was hard. But because we held the same goal of becoming emotionally and relationally connected, we built a bridge plowing through emotional fear. We pulled back the curtain on the things the other had done which upset us, caused us pain, or made us angry. I brought up my perceptions and feelings on how my mother reacted when my grandmother, my dad, and my brother died. She brought up her perceptions and feelings about when her mother, husband, and son died. Right there is an enormous clue. Although we both lost the same people, the relationships lost were *not* the same. Of course, our perceptions were different. We understood how deeply yet differently we'd suffered. The lies evaporated in light of the truth. Empathy built the bridge between us as we mourned for each other's losses, and understood each other's reactions, forgiving one another for hurting each other.

The relationship we built after building our bridge was beyond my wildest dreams, and we could've missed it if we hadn't owned a larger view where we were both right. Both my mother and I had skewed perceptions. We thought our perceptions were the only view. We thought we knew what the other was thinking. We were wrong. There was a larger view.

My mother and I developed a close relationship. She loved my husband and children well. We went on her dream vacation to Hershey, Pennsylvania at Christmas time together. We stood together in prayer as she bravely fought pancreatic cancer for fourteen months after being told she only had three to six months to live. I had the honor of sharing her last days with her. The Spirit of Grace answered my prayer by allowing me to be with her, holding her hand as she left her body and moved to heaven.

Where will owning a larger view benefit you? Owning a larger view takes a bit of humility. It's difficult to admit your perspective is skewed by your perception and might not be right. It might feel right or true. But it might not actually *be* true. Or it might be *partially* true.

Perceptions can lie. They can lie because there can be wounds in the way of seeing the truth. They're like dirt on a windshield that hinders correct vision, or like walking into a dark room where you think you see something, and there isn't anything there once you turn the light on.

Owning a larger view begins with questions and welcomes other people's perspectives.

OWN YOUR QUESTIONS: ANSWERS ARE AVAILABLE

Questions are the tools of the explorer; they are the treasure maps and flashlights of the heart hunter. By them we find the trails and tunnels into the inner life of another human heart.

—Sam Williamson

There are reasons for things, and questions are the tools to find the answers. Growing up, I was stifled from asking questions. Growing up in an authoritarian environment breeds compliant adults . . . unless there's rebellion. Parents, teachers, and leaders have a right to exercise their authority, but not to the squashing of individuals' right to understand. Blind obedience breeds trouble.

It's true, questions can be used for bad. For example, if someone doesn't like something going on, they might use questions to start a fight, undermine authority, or to manipulate the circumstance. (The Pharisees did this to Jesus all the time.) That's using the tool of questions for bad. The Bible tells us in James chapter four it's because we have wrong motives or fail to ask that we don't get the answers we're looking for.

Using questions out of a pure heart is a good thing. A pure heart seeking truth using questions is wise. The Bible puts wisdom and understanding together. *Wisdom is the principal thing; therefore, get wisdom: and with all thy getting get understanding.* How do we get wisdom and understanding if not to ask questions?

Sometimes our questions need adjusting. Sometimes our perspective is off, and we *ask the wrong question.* Jesus demonstrated this also. *Walking down the street, Jesus saw a man blind from birth. His disciples asked, "Rabbi, who sinned: this man or his parents, causing him to be born blind?" Jesus said, "****You're asking the wrong question. You're looking for someone to blame****. There is no such cause-effect here.* **Look instead for what God can do.** *We need to be energetically at work for the One who sent me here, working while the sun shines. When night falls, the workday is over. For as long as I am in the world, there is plenty of light. I am the world's Light."* (Emphasis mine) I don't believe the disciples had wrong motives in their question. Their perception was skewed by the law of Moses. Jesus responded by correcting their perspective.

If you're not finding answers in your seeking, then try adjusting the question—adjust your view.

By utilizing questions, you can find the answers you're looking for.

OWN YOUR CURIOSITY: QUESTIONS ARE HOW WE LEARN

We keep moving forward, opening new doors, and doing new things, because we're curious and curiosity keeps leading us down new paths.

—Walt Disney

There are negative attitudes in the world about curiosity; for example, *"curiosity killed the cat,"* or asking questions is being nosey. It's true there are times when questioning things is not prudent or goes too far, but curiosity is a good thing. Curiosity asks questions, and questions are how we learn. It's only those who feel threatened by them that shut them down. Many authority figures associate questions with rebellion. While it's true there are rebels, questions in and of themselves aren't bad. It's who or what's behind the question that makes the difference. What's their motive? Are they curious or something else? For example, the devil uses questions to trip people up. He's not curious, he's evil. His questions aren't. We only feel threatened by them when we're unsure of the answer. Jesus used questions also. Jesus is good. He used questions to reveal the hearts of the listeners so they would learn.

Questions are tools. Here are some examples of how to use them:

Asking questions when you meet people is how you get to know them. Do you have a new friend or boss who is introverted? Ask some curious questions to get them to talk about themselves. People like to talk about themselves.

Asking questions when you're taking a class is how you clarify things. Sometimes we can fail to ask questions in a learning situation because we're afraid to look stupid. But there may be another person in the same class longing for someone to ask the same question you have. If you choose to be courageous and speak up, you not only get your answer but might be helping someone else.

Journalists ask questions to get a story or get to the bottom of one. It's true they can take it too far. Or maybe I've watched too much television. But when you see something that doesn't seem like it fits, a curious question can bring an answer to shed light.

Own your curiosity to learn. Learn about yourself. Learn about your friends. Learn about your family. Learn about the world around you. Learn about the God who created you, and loves you. There is so much to learn in this life.

When I was growing up, I didn't have a thirst for learning as I do now. That's because my curiosity was stifled by shutting down my questions. Become thirsty to learn. Sometimes our questions lead to more questions. Like digging for fossils in a quarry, you can continue to dig for the truth and grow more than you ever imagined. Using curiosity to learn and grow can be fun.

Be curious and dig for treasures of wisdom, knowledge, and understanding.

OWN HOW YOU SEE YOURSELF

How can I believe there's a butterfly inside you or me when all I see is a fuzzy worm?

—Trina Paulus

We all have an opinion of ourselves. When we look at ourselves, we see an image. Maybe not visually or consciously, but we do, and it subconsciously drives our lives. For example, when I struggled with eating disorders, I saw myself as fat. I went through many different diets. I starved myself living on thirty calories a day until I became bulimic. I measured every part of my body obsessively—my chest, bust, waist, belly, hips, butt, thighs, biceps, and calves. I wrote it down to police myself. This went on for years. After becoming free of that mindset, it's clear I never was fat. It was fear and self-loathing.

If we're unhappy with who we are, and what's happening in our lives, we can change it. One crucial area is this self-opinion. Our view of our self. Are you aware of how you see yourself?

We live in an imperfect world where bad things happen. Everyone's situation and life challenges are different, but all of us suffer being treated improperly. In your lifetime someone won't like you and will say mean things to you or about you. Many are traumatized by this as children, and it distorts how the mind processes stimuli. Our perception of ourselves becomes skewed. Children blame themselves for the trauma they endure. When this self-blame goes unaddressed, it carries into adulthood with a negative self-opinion.

A person who repeatedly makes self-harming decisions, or practices self-harming behaviors has an unaddressed issue leaking into their life. The good news is this can be changed by changing how you see yourself.

Sometimes we need others to help us do this. They can help us see ourselves differently by showing us the value they see in us. For example, a woman named Deborah in the movie *Same Kind of Different as Me* changed many people's lives by showing them the respect and love they didn't give themselves. Many organizations do this also. Grace Centers of Hope in Pontiac, Michigan, for example, help men, women, and children, to see their value and reclaim their lives, from addiction and homelessness. The success stories are exciting to hear as they'll say things like *I never saw myself finishing school, owning a home, or having a decent job until I came here.* But they changed how they saw themselves, and it changed what they became.

Owning how you see yourself today will locate your starting point. Owning how you want to see yourself is how you become it.

Change on the outside begins with owning what you see on the inside.

OWN YOUR FINANCES: WEALTH BEGINS IN THE MIND

And God is able to bless you abundantly, so that in all things at all times, having all that you need, you will abound in every good work.

—Paul

This book isn't about money and finances, but finances are an important part of life. Because of this, I want to touch on taking ownership of your finances. The area of money is a place where many people feel like powerless victims. They'll focus on how they didn't grow up with any or how good—or bad—the economy is. They look to their past, or current situation, and disqualify themselves from the limitless supply that's available. Yes, I said limitless. Hear me out. You may think wealth is about money alone, but there's more to it. Wealth begins, resides, and emanates, from inside you. Let's look at the opposite: poverty.

Poverty is a mentality of insufficiency, inadequacy, scarcity, lack, and failure. Because we become how we see ourselves, a poverty mentality perpetuates the lack it perceives, in whatever area it sees it.

I used to have a poverty mentality. I saw lack everywhere. I had no comprehension of enough, let alone limitless supply. I saw a lack in who I was, how I felt, how I thought, how I talked, how I thought I should behave, in my relationships, in how I raised my kids, in where we lived, what we ate, in my relationship with God . . . It permeated every area of my life, and I felt trapped by it. But there was one thing I didn't lack. I didn't lack the stubbornness that says, *"where there's a will, there's a way."* Stubbornness produced hope because I wanted change in my life so desperately. I didn't know what a poverty mindset was. I just knew I was miserable and other people weren't. I was determined to find out how to grow and change. I hoped God would help, and He did.

God showed me the source of my problem was in my mind. In what I thought and believed. I believed I wasn't good enough to ever have enough, but God told me His grace was enough, and He'd teach me the right way to think. Changing how I thought began with finding out what God thought. The Bible says, *Beloved, I wish **above all things** that thou mayest **prosper** and be in health, even as thy soul prospereth. And you shall remember the Lord your God, for **it is He who gives you power to get wealth**, that He may establish His covenant which He swore to your fathers, as it is this day.* (emphasis mine)

At first, I'd look at my circumstances, and my insides would argue. God taught me I needed to take my focus off my circumstances and put my trust in Him. When the Bible said God is the source of wealth, and He wants me to have abundance through His grace, I needed to believe Him. That was no small task. Then God led my husband and me to tithe. We had questions and fear, but God asked us to trust. That's what tithing is, an act of trust. To me, it was *putting my money where my mouth was.* I could say I trusted God, but if I didn't trust Him with my money, I didn't really trust Him. It was through tithing we took ownership of our finances and handed them to God, who's the source of limitless supply. He promises to supply all our needs in every area. It was a journey. We fell off the wagon a few times. But now we take great joy in not only tithing but giving in multiple areas.

The Bible says to have a generous heart and how generosity brings God joy. It tells us when we give it's multiplied back to us.

It's not magic. It's a journey of changing how we think, who we're trusting, and where the source of our supply is. When our past, or our circumstances, are our source, we'll come up short. But if we'll let God be our source, the possibilities are endless. Not everyone needs the same things, and people balk against this truth because of stupid things others have done in the name of God.

There is plenty of wealth on this planet for everyone, but greed and a poverty mindset get in the way. Those who don't get caught in them are generous givers. They get to participate in this promise from the Bible: *You will be enriched in every way so that you can be generous on every occasion, and through us,* **your generosity will result in thanksgiving to God.** (emphasis mine) Imagine such abundance. True wealth is in taking ownership of your finances and handing them to God.

How we own our mindset will bring abundance or scarcity.

OWN YOUR *INSTEAD* TO CHANGE YOUR LIFE

If you can turn it around in your heart and in your mouth — you can turn it around in your situation.

—Gloria Copeland

Instead is a powerful word. It means substitute or alternative. Using the power of instead is a way you can change your life. The power of instead works like an interception. In football, an interception changes the direction of the game. It interrupts the momentum. Just one interception has the power to change the outcome of the game.

Here is how I first learned the power of instead. I used to suffer horrible disorienting confusion. I hated it. I wanted it to change and cried out to God to help me. He gave me a specific arrangement of words to reprogram my mind. These words interrupted the self-attacking negative thought process I had going on in the back of my mind. The instructions I received along with the words were to rehearse them out loud daily. These are the words I was given: *There is <u>no</u> <u>condemnation</u> for Me who is in Christ Jesus. It is for freedom that Christ has <u>set</u> <u>me</u> <u>free.</u> The one who is throwing me into confusion will pay the penalty, whoever he may be. <u>That</u> kind of persuasion does not come from the one who calls me. But the fruit of the spirit is love, joy, peace, patience, kindness, goodness, faithfulness, gentleness, and self-control. Against such things there is no law.*

After a while of rehearsing these words daily, when a thought of confusion or condemnation came to my mind, I'd answer them with those words. Doing this *intercepted* my habit of running off at the mouth with negative words against myself that agreed with the condemnation and confusion like I used to before. I started to call them *instead* words when I realized I was speaking the words God had given me to speak, *instead* of what I felt and *instead* of what I'd always said before. Those words drove the debilitating confusion out of my mind and gave me a mind at peace—*instead*. It was the beginning of me embracing the *sound mind* God says is available.

Here's an example from the world of technology of what we do when we use the power of instead on our minds:

I was watching a TV program with my husband where a team of special operatives went to a foreign country to retrieve a discarded hard drive. The files on the hard drive had been deleted but were in the hands of a man running a salvage operation where they knew how to get access to sensitive files that had been deleted, and then blackmail the owner. (Seems that's really a thing going on in our world.) There are two ways to protect yourself. One is to destroy the hard drive (like with a sledgehammer) or use the power of instead. Using the power of *instead* is rewriting over the digital copy that had been deleted. Without doing this, these deleted files are not really gone. Writing over them is the only way to permanently delete the original file.

It's the same with our minds. We don't want to destroy our minds, and trying to not think about things embedded in our psyche doesn't work. It takes rewriting new copy with *instead* words and behaviors to free us from the old mental programming. Utilizing this power of *instead* takes work. But it's good work, and it's guaranteed to change the direction of your life. Our lives go in the direction of our prevailing thoughts. When we change our prevailing thoughts by rewriting over the old, we change the direction our life is going.

Is there a place where your life is being derailed?

Own your *instead* and reprogram your mind to alter your course.

KEY POINTS

- Mindsets can be positive or negative and subject to emotional triggers.
- Perception is the way in which you process information. It's a filter. It's part of your mindsets or mental pathways.
- Negative mindsets cause condemnation and confusion.
- There are times when two perspectives seem to clash, yet both are true.
- A pure heart seeking truth using questions is wise.
- Using curiosity to learn and grow can be fun.
- Change on the outside begins with owning what you see on the inside.
- How we own our mindset will bring abundance or scarcity.
- The power of *instead* works like an interception and rewriting over digital copy.

YOU CAN ASK GOD FOR HELP

Thank you for my mind, God. It's such a powerful tool. Help me to grab ahold of it in all the different areas. Help me learn, grow, and live abundantly like you promised.

NOTES

How Mary Took Ownership Of Her Life

Sometimes life reveals the path to you. You have a choice about whether you're going to take that path.

—Mary O'Donohue

I had the pleasure of meeting Mary at the 2018 Tribe Writer's Conference in Franklin, Tennessee. Mary has worked in the media industry for years and carries herself with quiet confidence. When I learned she worked with Oprah for many years, I could have easily been intimidated, but Mary is a welcoming soul with the desire to help others. I had the honor of being mentored by her through her Media Savvy Author group. Mary is a courageous woman who's owned many opportunities life has offered her.

Opportunities arise for all of us, but many times we shrink back in fear of the unknown. Certainly, Mary took advantage of opportunities early in her life, or she would never have worked with Oprah. But her commitment to saying yes to opportunities increased one sad day driving home from a friend's funeral. She took ownership of her grief through a promise that the next time an opportunity came along in her life that she knew she couldn't accomplish, she would do it anyway, for him.

This promise has motivated Mary to own multiple things. Shortly after the death of her friend, she got a call from an agent who was working with her sister. Mary had been developing a way to teach her children values, and this agent found out about it. *"The agent said, you know, this is a book, what you're doing with your kids is a book."* Mary was hesitant, but because of that promise, she took ownership of this new thing called writing a book. She reminded herself of the promise over and over throughout this new journey. Writing a book proposal was new and scary enough. Fear escalated when she got a phone call. *"My agent called and said, we have an offer, I was like, Oh, I can't write a book. I'm not a writer. But I had to remember the promise."*

Mary's book was published in 2010. *"It became a best seller and broke Amazon's top 100, which is very hard to do. And it won two awards. To this day, I am shocked about the fact that I would never ever have written the book, if not for the promise I made to my friend."*

The opportunity to write the book came and Mary could have passed it up—but she didn't. She owned it doing what she felt certain she was incapable of. Mary wasn't incapable, it was just fear. As Mary elaborated on this she shared how *"there's so much in life that we don't do, because we're sure we can't do it."* This has changed Mary's perspective on doing the impossible in life from *"I can't do this thing"* to *"how can I?"*

Three years after releasing her book Mary was diagnosed with a neurological disease testing her resolve to overcome the impossible. Her family moved into a new home and *"about three months later, I started getting sick, and having trouble standing. By 2014, I was needing to walk with a cane."*

Her health steadily grew worse as physical and neurological symptoms mimicking MS surfaced. Sometimes she couldn't speak because she couldn't think clearly. *"I would hold something up and say, you know, what is this called again, and my daughter would be like, 'that's a glass'. And I'd look at it and that word glass just had no familiarity to me."* She went to numerous doctors who offered little to no hope.

"I'm not a religious person at all, but I am a person of faith, I have a very personal faith." Even when she felt isolated and unable to pray, *"because I couldn't think of the words,"* Mary clung to her

faith, reminding herself she wasn't as alone as she felt. *"That was just terrifying, you know, so I would just sit, sometimes I would just sit, and feel like, I think I'm alone, but I'm not alone. So, I just need to remember that. And this is where I am."*

Mary held onto courage and strength throughout her health scare. Finally, she received a proper diagnosis. A doctor she'd known for years diagnosed her and treated her for mold illness. He had hope to offer. Mary did the treatments he prescribed, which caused a lot of fatigue. But *"about seven and a half months later, I could start to walk. And then you know, my brain came back."* Forever grateful to be well again Mary takes nothing for granted. Every day she seeks out opportunities to be kind and compassionate to others. It's who she is. Her kindness and giving heart were the pathway leading her to what she does now. But she didn't see it at first.

At a conference for doctors, a psychologist friend of Mary's texted her about a doctor who was in attendance. *"There's this wonderful and amazing doctor here, who I think would benefit from a media coach. Could you media coach her?"* Mary had never seen herself as a media coach and balked, but her friend persisted, so Mary accepted the challenge.

Mary began her coaching work via Skype while she was still recovering and using a cane. It went so well that people started hearing about her skills and referrals were streaming in. She didn't start with a curriculum but developed one as she went. She worked with a variety of clients and started to develop classes. As her media coaching evolved, her connection to authors became apparent. Specifically, nonfiction authors. *"I'm also a nonfiction author. So, I think that I understand the author's journey."* Mary compares the nonfiction authors journey to climbing a mountain, and I agree. The process involves preparation, resistance, fear, exertion, and exhilaration. Helping others climb their mountain to bring their pain, their victory, their journey, their lessons to market to help others, brings Mary much joy. *"There's something I think, very unselfish and beautiful about the heart of a nonfiction author and very generous. I love working with people like that and want to make someone else's journey as an author easier."*

As Mary's been growing her media coaching business, she's also had the opportunity to work with many of her former colleagues from the Oprah show on other projects. Every project Mary works on, and every interview she watches, she gathers more knowledge and skill for her students. She sees things from her media mind that non media people (like me) miss. *"Everything sort of comes home to media for me."*

Mary exudes confidence, and her students benefit greatly from it. She instills that confidence and courage into them. Her path in life is clear right now. Something she shared with me is when she knew her direction, doors would open for her. It happened with her book and it happened with her media coaching. *"All I needed was the courage to walk through the doors, because I didn't know where those doors were taking me. But they're open."*

Mary walked through the open door to write her book. She walked through the door to a different therapy to treat her illness. And again, she walked through the door of opportunity to become a media coach. This is how we get to new levels of growth in our lives.

When we follow the path life offers us and we climb our mountains, we see from a different perspective and it enlarges our worldview. We might think we're doing it only for ourselves, but the truth is because of our newfound understanding we can help others also. We do this in simple conversation as well as in sharing through more intentional ways like writing a book. *"And so how does that help? Because at the end of the day Danielle what's so fascinating to me is that, there are people helped by your book, there are people helped by my book, and those people don't get helped unless we step up and have the courage to put our experiences in a book and get it out into the world."*

Mary enjoys being a media coach who teaches nonfiction authors how to get publicity without a publicist and do game-changing media interviews. This is how she helps them get their message out into the world. She understands how difficult the process is both practically and emotionally. Mary encourages people to climb their mountain of writing a book. Once they've succeeded, she helps them release their message in the most powerful way to do the most good. *"Writing a book is like holding a flock of birds and releasing them into the world. And they're going to go anywhere and everywhere and carry your message. There are people out there who are hurting for your message, are healed by your message, are inspired, are educated—all of that. When we're able to release our imperfect message into the world, it's life-changing for people we'll never meet. And that is the thing that so affects me. Because when we stay small and say 'I can't do these things'. We think we're hurting our own lives. But it's more than that. We're hurting the lives of people we'll never meet. So, I feel like if we think about it as 'what can I do for others imperfectly', then I think all of us can do great things."*

Find out more about Mary and what she has to offer in the endnotes.

CHAPTER 10

Owning Grace

Living loved, we relax our expectations, our efforts, our strivings, our rules, our spine, our breath, our plans, our job descriptions and checklists; we step off the treadmill of the world and the treadmill of religious performance. We are not the authors of our redemption.

—Sarah Bessey

HOW TO BEGIN

Owning your life is a life-long endeavor involving many things. Grace is critical to your success. Why? Because you'll have trouble along the way, and grace is what will give you the power to continue in the face of difficulty or disappointment. Grace reminds you, you're human. Grace empowers you to *not* expect perfection of yourself. Perfectionism is destructive. The only thing perfect is God, and His grace can make all the difference in our lives. I know it does in mine. This may sound simplistic because the power of grace can elude us. It eluded me for a long time. I knew it as a religious term. I was familiar with how the Bible says we're *saved by grace*. But I didn't grasp the magnitude of grace until the Spirit of Grace showed me it's the all-powerful goodness of God toward us.

I dare you to discover and own the all-powerful grace of God for you.

OWN THE GRACE THAT DEEMED YOU WORTHY OF LOVE

We love him, because he first loved us.

—John

Being loved and loving others is the core need in each of us. Yet, this need often goes unmet. In fact, feeling unloved is rampant in our world. Why do we fail to feel love? Because we fail to *believe* we're loved. Feeling loved, or not, is a result of what we believe. This means we have power over something, where we think we don't. What other people think and do is their decision. What we think and do is ours.

For a long time, I measured my lovability by others. This is no way to live. No human is perfect. We know this in the *I understand English* sort of way but acting like it's true is another story. This is what leads us to believe we're unworthy of love. We feel we're not good enough. When we measure ourselves against the standard of perfection, we fall short every single time.

But there's another way. Grace. Yes, it's true we're not perfect all by ourselves, but we have the option to not be all by ourselves. God, who created us, loves us and has provided grace. His grace has deemed us worthy of love. This grace has provided the perfection we crave and need. This grace is ours in Jesus. I love how it says in the Bible, *the law was given by Moses, but grace and truth came by Jesus.* The law is what feeds our mindset of inferiority. It's the measure of perfection no one can attain. It was *given* by

Moses. Giving something can be done impersonally and far away. For example, I could mail you a gift. But the grace providing the perfection we need *came*. Jesus *came*. It's different from a gift. It's personal. Jesus personally came to give you His grace because He deems you worthy of His love.

Seizing the grace of God says *I receive your esteem of me.*

OWN YOUR HUMANITY: MISTAKES ARE A PART OF LIFE

Each life is made up of mistakes and learning, waiting and growing, practicing patience and being persistent.

—Billy Graham

Learning to make mistakes was a game-changer for me. Let me explain. My inner critic was a tyrant. Whenever I made a mistake, fell short of what I felt obligated to do or perform, my insides would react as if it was the end of the world. The self-condemnation was brutal. Due to the spiritual trauma in my life, I believed God was mad at me too. For me to break out of this mindset, it took an encounter with the Spirit of Grace, telling me He was going to teach me how to make mistakes. I freaked. He went on to explain mistakes are part of being human. He assured me, He knew I would make another mistake, and it wouldn't be the end of the world. I understood what He was telling me, but it took time to work this new way of thinking into me. Perfectionism and overbearing, demanding, authority figures make mistakes seem fatal. It's a lie. It's fed by fear. Admitting your humanity will free you from the bondage of that lie.

Mistakes can be quite useful. For me to say that is evidence of how far I've come. They're learning tools if we'll allow them to play teacher. Thomas Edison, as he perfected his invention of the light bulb, is a great example. Each version that didn't work—or failed—he used to learn what didn't work and tried something else.

When we learn from our mistakes, they simply become part of our journey through life.

Living life, expecting yourself to never fail and disallowing mistakes, is to dehumanize yourself. Instead, own your humanity and give yourself grace.

We can call for grace too. Like God told Zerubbabel to, *". . . with shoutings, crying 'Grace! Grace!'"* and the God of all grace hears us and responds. When we call for it, all His powerful goodness is invited into the situation. He'll help us learn and grow. The Bible tells us: *. . . in all things God works for the good of those who love him, who have been called according to his purpose.*

Grace gives us the power to embrace our mistakes and allow God to make use of them.

OWN YOUR NEEDS: HAVING NEEDS IS HUMAN

God shall supply all your need according to his riches in glory by Christ Jesus.

—Paul

For some, when I say having needs is human, they reply with "duh." But for others, like me, it's a learning process. When your needs have been dismissed, unmet, or violated, it's damaging. It cripples you because having needs *is* human, normal, and natural. The difference between needs and wants can be difficult to navigate. It was for me; and to be transparent, I sometimes still struggle.

There are different kinds of needs too: Physical, emotional, relational, educational, vocational, spiritual . . . etc. Needs aren't the same for everyone. Yes, there're some we all share, like the need to eat and breathe. Real basic. But needs coincide with who we are, where we live, and what path we have to travel in life. For example, a farmer needs a tractor while a businesswoman in New York will not; a lawyer needs a suit while an artist might not; a person who lives in Minnesota needs a winter coat while someone in Arizona won't. You get the idea.

Needs can change, too. What we need today may not be what we need in a year. A newborn baby, for example, needs to be fed and changed; but, the baby becomes a child who can feed themselves and use the toilet. Needs change with growth. Another example is when someone falls down and hurts themselves, they may need to cry; but, as they move into healing the crying will no longer be needed. Needs change with healing.

By owning your needs, you can embrace growth and healing. Needs are evidence of life. Plants need light and water. Why? To grow. Living things grow. Growing things change. Embrace your humanity and the needs that go with it in your life, regardless of where you are on your journey of healing, growth, or change. Then you can become your true self. You'll be empowered to fulfill whatever God has called you to do.

Own your needs, voice them to God, and allow Him to supply them.

OWN THE BIGNESS OF GOD

Each time he said, "My grace is all you need. My power works best in weakness." So now I am glad to boast about my weaknesses, so that the power of Christ can work through me.

—Paul

We can be blinded by our weaknesses. They can feel so big they make God look small. But it's a lie that's after your hope. It wants to shame you into depression and make you feel helpless. Victory can be found in owning the bigness of God and the help He offers.

We need to remind ourselves we're not alone, and there's no shame in weakness. When we own the bigness of God, we take our weakness and hand it to Him, because we know He's more than enough to deal with it. It's in our union with God, we become powerful. Alone, we are weak—even when we feel strong. Our strength is nothing compared to God's. In fact, our *strength* gets in the way of Him helping us. When we reach for self-reliance instead of the assistance of the Spirit of Grace—also known as the anointing—He can't help us. It's like saying *no thank you. I got it.* God's on our side and desires to help us. But He won't force Himself on us. It's our choice. The Bible says *we can do all things through Christ who gives us strength.* That's partnership with His anointing. The Bible also tells us, *His anointing has the power to not only break yokes (bondages, burdens) but to destroy them.*

If you want to own His bigness, close your eyes and imagine the bigness of the Almighty God, how He created the universe, how He created our world, how *He holds it all together with His word.* Imagine that bigness on your side, helping you. It's a powerful vision. It begins in conceiving it in your mind, choosing to believe His bigness loves you and is *on your side* to help you.

David, in the book of Psalms, gives us a picture of how to own God's bigness through worship. *Oh, magnify the LORD with me, And let us exalt His name together.* When you're aware of His bigness and love for you, your weakness is a non-issue, and you'll overcome. It may be quick or take a long time. But the end is sure when we rely on Him and all He is. Jesus said, *"Come to me you who are weary and heavy laden, and I will give you rest."*

When you own the bigness of God, you can rest in His strength and supply.

OWN THE FAITHFULNESS OF GOD

If we believe not, yet he abideth faithful: he cannot deny himself.

—Timothy

The above scripture, from Second Timothy, carried me through many a dark day when I found unbelief in me instead of faith. I struggled to believe God was faithful because I saw everything that was wrong in my life, instead of what He was doing.

Things happen in life that reveal how much faith we really have. Situations will arise suddenly, like a storm. It's not doomsday, it's reality. When things happen that we aren't expecting, they shake us up, spin us around, and overwhelm our mind and emotions.

It's easy to believe God is faithful when things are calm. It's when the pain is overwhelming, and we can't see straight, we discover what's in our hearts because it comes out our mouths. Sometimes, we shock ourselves . . . like Simon Peter. He was a disciple of Jesus and *denied knowing Jesus with swearing, just as Jesus had predicted.* Peter was cut to the heart when he realized what he'd done. He really wanted to believe Jesus but discovered his faith was found lacking. Jesus didn't respond with condemnation, like we tend to do to ourselves, but with abundant grace.

I've had my faith shaken, and it's scary. When our faith gets shaken, we question what we believe about everything—about God, ourselves, and life. But there's hope. There's grace to hold onto our faith amid being shaken.

Faith is putting your trust in something, or someone. When your faith is being shaken, the trust is being put on trial for how strong it is. When you feel your faith is lacking, here are three things I've discovered to hold onto. They're like an anchor that'll get you through the storm:

ONE – Stick with what you know. Recalling scriptures, answered prayers, and your history with God are examples of what I mean when I say stick with what you know. They can quiet the raging questions: *what if, what about, and why.* Simon Peter did this. He remembered the grace, mercy, and kindness of Jesus. He remembered how the Father *had revealed to him that Jesus was the Son of the living God.*

TWO – Have faith in God. I picture this as reaching for God like a child reaches for a parent when they're scared. Prayer, worship, and simply choosing to believe He's bigger than the storm we see raging, are ways we can reach for Him. Reaching is a demonstration of faith. When Simon Peter denied Jesus, he remembered how *Jesus had not only predicted his failure but prayed for Peter that his faith wouldn't fail.* Peter *chose to have faith in God. He believed Jesus was bigger than His denial.* Jesus was indeed bigger, and *not only reconciled Peter but asked him to help others.*

THREE – Reach for help. When our faith is lacking, it's good to ask for help. Asking others to pray for us and seeking the counsel of a friend or pastor are good examples of reaching out. The Bible tells us that *two are better than one.* You're not alone, so don't let yourself be. Consider the Bible giant John the Baptist. Jesus said no one arose greater, yet John found himself in a place where his faith was lacking. When he was in jail, he *questioned if Jesus was really the Messiah.* John reached out to his own disciples, asking for help, who went to Jesus for answers. John was met with encouragement so he could stick with what he knew to begin with – *"Look, the Lamb of God, who takes away the sin of the world!"* and, *"I have seen, and I testify that this is God's Chosen One."*

There's no condemnation when you find yourself weak in faith. How many times did Jesus ask the disciples *why do you have so little faith?* But continued to help them. When our faith is lacking, it's simply our humanity in the process of becoming fully persuaded in the faithfulness of God. The grace of God will carry us through, just like the first disciples. When your faith is shaken, don't condemn yourself. God doesn't. Hang on, His grace will see you through.

You can own His faithfulness through His grace.

OWN SONGS OF DELIVERANCE: MUSIC CARRIES HEALING AND POWER

You are my hiding place; you will protect me from trouble and surround me with songs of deliverance.

—David

It's said music is the language of emotion. As a teenager, I certainly connected with music in my coming of age sorrow. Many teens do. It's not uncommon to hear stories of young people retreating to their rooms to escape into whatever music speaks the emotions going on in their soul. This connection can be harnessed for good. For example, a young man named David played music for a king named Saul in the Bible. Saul would become troubled, and David would be summoned. David referred to this power as *songs of deliverance*. David used these *songs of deliverance* also *when he was running from that same king who was now trying to kill him*.

I've benefited from the power of *songs of deliverance*. Sometimes they've come to me by grace alone. Meaning, just when I needed it, the Spirit of Grace provided the song I needed. Other times I happened to remember it, think about it, by "coincidence" it would be playing wherever I happened to be, or someone would send it to me. For example, when my husband and I moved to Arizona. He went ahead of me, and I stayed home to sell the house. I was excited about this new adventure but also more scared than I admitted to myself. I started having panic attacks and ended up on medication. The first of many *songs of deliverance* dealing with this time in my life was *Brave* by Gavin Mikhail. Someone I didn't know dropped it on my social media page and I owned it. This *song of deliverance* became oxygen to my soul. There were many others the Spirit of Grace gave me during that difficult time in my life.

To tap into the power of *songs of deliverance* they don't have to come to you. You can go looking for them. For example, look through your music library, do a search online, or ask a friend. *Songs of deliverance* fill your heart with good words of encouragement. They uplift, strengthen, and empower you. The music carries the healing past your ears, into your soul. When the songs have words from the Spirit of Grace, they're even more powerful.

Music and words bring powerful deliverance carried on the winds of grace.

KEY POINTS

- Grace is what'll give you the power to continue in the face of difficulty or disappointment.
- Seizing the grace of God says *I receive your esteem of me.*
- Grace gives us the power to embrace our mistakes and allow God to make use of them.
- Needs coincide with who we are, where we live, and what path we have to travel in life.
- When you own the bigness of God, you can rest in His strength and supply.
- When our faith is lacking, it's simply our humanity in the process of becoming fully persuaded in the faithfulness of God. The grace of God will carry us through, just like the first disciples.
- Music and words bring powerful deliverance, carried on the winds of grace.

YOU CAN ASK GOD FOR HELP

God of all grace help me embrace all of your powerful goodness. Help me to see grace as more than just a religious term, but your power at work in my life because you love me.

NOTES

How Tom Took Ownership Of His Life

If it works for you, it's the right way to do it.

—Tom Shea

Tom is an extraordinary man. We met when I lived in Arizona. Had he not told me; I never would've thought he was disabled in any way. Tom was born with cerebral palsy and undiagnosed Asperger's. When he was a baby, the doctor told his mother, he would never walk. Tom's mother refused to believe it. Where Tom is now, and what he's accomplished is beyond remarkable.

In my interview with Tom, he told me how doctors used to separate Asperger's from Autism when he was first diagnosed at the age of forty-six. But *"these days in the diagnostic world they've lumped them together as one disorder, and it's called Autism Spectrum Disorder."* Tom refers to it as simply Autism and told me one of the characteristics is having a fascination with one or two subjects. For Tom, it's sports (particularly baseball) and contemporary jazz music.

One of the first things that impressed me about Tom is how he took ownership of who he is and how he processes information. When having a conversation with him and something he associates with the autism takes place, he points it out and sometimes chuckles. He's comfortable in his own skin. I find that amazing. Here is a man who would have all the reasons to be uncomfortable, but he's not. His positive nature was instilled in him by his mother early in his life.

Positive nature is really an understatement. What Tom was given by his mother was a profound treasure that gave him the power to take ownership of his life. I'm flabbergasted at this woman. She was audacious, courageous, and tenacious. Understand, Tom was born in the fifties. Back then, *"women did not go against doctors in the white coats and tell the doctors what they can do with their stethoscope."*

A few years ago, Tom told me the story of the first time he crawled. He was about two years old. Before that, his mom had been told to 'just buy him a wheelchair.' Instead, she worked with him at home using a creative and progressive technique to cause his brain to register the nerve response. Her friends didn't approve. She didn't care. Tom's dad built a box three inches high, and they filled it with crushed granite. They put railings on either side for Tom to hold onto. *"My mom would kneel in front of me. She would grab my bare ankles, my bare feet, grinding them against the gravel in a walking motion, and it would hurt."* Over and over and over, she did this. Until the day it happened. Tom was in the living room, and he saw an extension cord. It captivated him and he went to go get it—crawling for the first time. Tom's mom scooped him into her arms, grabbed the extension cord, and drove to the doctor's office where she burst into a patient's room to see the doctor. As they were all objecting to her behavior, she launched the cord down the hall, placed Tom gently on the floor and exclaimed, "Watch!" as Tom happily crawled to the extension cord. Jaws dropped. The impossible just took place.

Although crawling was an amazing milestone, Tom dreamed of walking, and his mother was right there with him. In the interview, Tom shared his incredible story. *"She just wouldn't take no for an answer. And this is how far she took it."*

Tom's mom took him for therapy at an Easter Seals clinic to work on walking when he was two. At the clinic, as he struggled to get his feet to work properly, his mother spoke to everyone in the room: doctors, therapists, everyone. She instructed them she wouldn't allow any negative words to be spoken while he was working. There would be no "you can't do that" or "it's too much of a struggle" or anything to get him to quit. She demanded that if they were going to say anything negative, they had to get out of the room. *"I don't want him to hear anything negative out of anyone's mouth."*

With his tiny hand gripping the bars, his feet dangled beneath him. On the floor laid a ladder. It had fire engine red and black rungs on it. Propped up on either end of the ladder were mirrors. When he struggled, he'd look to his mom for approval. She'd smile "keep going" then direct his attention to the mirrors. She wanted him to focus on the mirrors and not on her. The mirrors were for visual cues of where his feet were. When a foot went sideways, he could move it straight by seeing where it was, and then put it where it was supposed to go.

This grueling process went on and on for what felt like forever to Tom. His mom's friends abandoned and ostracized her telling her to get Tom a wheelchair and forget about all she was doing. But she ignored the negative. At the clinic, she made sure they never said anything negative to Tom.

"They didn't believe it would work. But they never said anything negative."

Tom walked out of the clinic unaided when he was seven!

"The last day of therapy, I walked down a stairway by myself, I held onto the railing. One step at a time. When I left, my mother made all the naysayers and the therapist that didn't think this was ever going to happen stand up at the top of the stairwell and watch me walk down the stairs. All the way to the first floor."

Little seven-year-old Tom took it slow. He didn't stumble or fall. All the way to the bottom with all the disbelievers watching. And then she gave them a verbal thrashing.

"Don't ever tell a child what they can and cannot do. You don't know what they can accomplish. And for you guys, for people, adults to talk it down because you think you know better is not right. Maybe they can't do it. Maybe they do have limitations. But you don't know where those limitations lie. And to not be able to become all you can be is not right. And to put negative thoughts and words into a kid's mind is a terrible thing to do. 'Oh, he'll never be able to do this. I don't know why he thinks he's so good.' You can't do that. That's like poison. Don't you ever do it to your future clients! Don't do that!"

Yes, Tom does have some limitations. But they're nowhere near where the professionals thought they were.

Tom developed the same attitude as his mother of 'not taking no for an answer.' In elementary school, he wanted to play sports. But because of the cerebral palsy and being almost legally blind in one eye he knew it wasn't going to happen. Instead of wallowing in self-pity he took ownership of what he could do. He got an idea.

With baseball as his favorite sport and living in a suburb of Chicago he set his sights on the Chicago Cubs. Maybe he could be their bat boy. He asked his parents' permission to write them. They said yes and he wrote a letter to John Holland.

"He was one of the big shots there back in the 60s."

John Holland wrote Tom back thanking him for his interest but said he lived too far from Wrigley Field. Although Tom was disappointed, he didn't let go of his dream to do something with sports.

Tom's family moved to Arizona. Soon after he got another idea. He wanted to be a ball boy for the Phoenix Suns. Once again, he wrote a letter. The only name he knew was Joe Proski who was their trainer. This time Tom felt he had leverage though. He discovered his dad's employer was the Sun's biggest sponsor. In his letter he was certain to mention that key fact. But they blew him off. Undaunted, Tom called Mr. Proski's office repeatedly for months saying how he wrote a letter and asking for a response. Every time he'd get the same *"he'll get to his mail"* answer. Tom was getting frustrated when he got an opportunity.

"They had a situation at the Coliseum where they were filming a movie. They asked people to come down there to be fans in the stands. Because it was a basketball themed movie and they needed people to cheer. So, if you come, we'll give you three tickets to a Suns game. I'm there."

After the game he saw Mr. Proski and went to talk with him. Tom recalls him saying *"Oh, yeah, you're the guy whose dad works for our biggest sponsor. I can't do anything with you. But let me introduce you to Ted Podleski."* They took his contact information and said they'd get back to him.

Before the season started, they called while he was in school. They asked his mother if he could come down to try out for the position of ball boy. Tom made his parents promise to drive him if he got the job. Secretly thinking he wouldn't, they promised. But Tom got the job! There were forty-one home games at the Coliseum he'd need a ride to and from. *"I was thrilled I got hired. I go 'mom you get to drive me to the Coliseum tonight and Wednesday and Friday and Sunday'. I was thrilled but she didn't smile."*

His mother's audacious, courageous tenaciousness operating in Tom empowered him to realize his dream. By it he was hired for other jobs also. For example, in an interview for a check cashing job. *"When I was in the interview for that situation. I had the guts to tell the owner who hired me, I said to his face 'This is one of the smartest things you've ever done, I'm gonna be the best employee you've ever had. You just don't know it yet.' When I went to leave, he called me into his office. He waited in his office for three hours because he wanted to talk to me so bad. And he said, 'I just want you to know, Tom that, seven years ago when you told me that you'd be the best employee. I thought that was gutsy, this kid. You know what, Tom, you were right. You're absolutely right. I wish you well, as you go on in your career. You're the best employee I've ever hired."*

Tom also worked for an MLB team (the Arizona Diamondbacks) running their parking department. For three years he managed their garages, oversaw thirty teenage guys, and dealt with drunken fans. Not bad for a guy who wasn't supposed to be able to crawl. Eh?

But not every interview Tom went on went like that. There were times when the symptoms of his Autism got the best of him before he knew the cause. *"I couldn't figure out why I couldn't do these things."* But because he knew he needed a job and that required going on interviews, he pressed through and got better with practice.

When Tom was diagnosed with Asperger's Syndrome, he was relieved. All the things he thought made him strange: inability to pick up social cues and maintain eye contact, meltdowns, literalness, and black/white thinking, made sense now. All this time he had a disability and didn't know it. Tom looks back and gives God the credit for all he's accomplished and for the mom he had. *"God gave me the right mother. If I hadn't had the mother I had, you probably wouldn't have met me, I'd be in a wheelchair in some rehab place somewhere. I don't know, doing whatever you do. So, you know, God is at the top. God gave me my mother. He knew just who it should be."*

There is so much more to Tom's story I can't possibly share it all. Fifteen years ago, Tom struggled interacting in a small group of ten. When I asked Tom if I could interview him for this book, he had just accomplished another milestone—public speaking. He sat in front of a group of thirty-five people talking about the aspects of Autism. He did this for forty-five minutes! He did it so well they invited him back. Tom was shocked but graciously accepted. As he walked out of the room and down the hall, Tom felt immense satisfaction, it felt wonderful, and he thanked God.

Tom shares his extraordinary positive outlook everywhere he goes. He knows his ability to ignore the negative is a gift he received from his mother and most people don't have that. He seeks to put positive energy into everyone he meets. *"I give them a little list. You're intelligent, you're beautiful, you're kind, you're loving, you're helpful, whatever positive attributes that I know that they have, and I verbalize them back to them so they hear it. I want that to go into their ears. Like my mother didn't want the negative to come into mine. So, I put the positive into theirs. I know, I'm a one-man band, but whatever seeds I can plant are worthy of being planted. Whether they germinate or not. It's not my job. So I don't worry about that. But I am going to constantly when I see people give them the positive instead of the negative out there. When you hear it enough over and over again, you'll start to believe it."*

If you're interested in connecting with Tom, in the print copy of this book, I have all the information for you to connect with him in the endnotes.

CHAPTER 11

Owning Your Process

To everything there is a season, and a time to every purpose under the heaven.

—Solomon

HOW TO BEGIN

In this chapter, I share the processes I've been through. I own them deeply and personally. I share them because they've radically changed my life. My greatest desire is to empower you to be your best self to live your best life. Remember *I am me and you are you.*[25] That may mean some of what worked for me will work differently for you. Or maybe there are things I did or believe that you're not interested in. Feel the freedom to take what works for you and discard what doesn't. This book is for you to take ownership of your life, not for me to tell you what to do. We're all unique, and no two journeys through any process will be identical, even if we take the same steps.

Everything has a process. Everything. It took me a long time to trust that. For example, when I was a teenager, my mom gave me a poster that said *Things take Time*. I hated it. I rejected the idea. Process and waiting were things I didn't understand. My emotions and thoughts had been mangled by trauma, and I wasn't aware of anything but pain. I wanted relief right now, not later, and definitely not a long procedure. My stubbornness and ignorance kept me trapped in the pain. But perceptions are our reality, even when they're inaccurate. At the beginning of any process, we're stuck with where we are at that time. We have to own that starting place, to begin to move forward.

I dare you to embrace the process you need in your life for your wholeness.

OWN WHERE YOU ARE: DARE TO BELIEVE YOU'LL SUCCEED

My times are in thy hand: deliver me from the hand of mine enemies, and from them that persecute me.

—David

Accepting where you are, and then daring to believe you can gain the success you're going after, is to begin your progression to wholeness. Entering this process says *you matter!* Love says *you're worth it.* Feeling unloved is an issue many deal with as well as a common byproduct of childhood and emotional trauma. It's why we have to dare to believe.

Love changes everything. Grace is love in action. If we can come to believe that we're loved, not just in our head but in our heart, we can see our value. Then we can move on to accept grace. Within grace is forgiveness. Grace silences the voice of shame and condemnation. Grace encourages you and helps you to get back up, every time you fall down. The grace we talked about in the previous chapter is a powerful tool to succeed through every process you need. Process does many things.

- Process begins.
- Process finds help.
- Process brings new thinking and creates new habits, which builds confidence.
- Process provides little victories.
- Process celebrates these victories and develops gratitude.

All of these help us to build trust as we progress in our journey. Process is a repetitive cycle. We can get frustrated when it takes longer than we want. I did. Many times, in my *"journey to emerge,"* I wept in that frustration. I was afraid it was taking so long because I was doing something wrong. I would beat myself up. But I wasn't doing anything wrong. My healing was a long progression due to the depth of the injury to my soul. The Spirit of Grace (**The Pursuer**) showed me a way to visualize this involved procedure. This helped me give myself grace. Here is the explanation as I wrote about it.

Microsurgery – I was pondering all the deep work in my soul that was being done, all the counseling etc. and this word came to me. I had to go and see if it was an actual word or actual medical thing – it is and it is amazing. **The Pursuer** *has been doing this in my heart. But I also learned that before microsurgery is performed there is a necessary preparation. This really spoke to me about my long process. One of the stories I read talked about a severe injury involving broken bones with open flesh that was contaminated by dirt, grass and whatnot. They had to remove the foreign materials, spray wash it with gallons of antibiotic fluid and then need to pack it with some kind of beads saturated with antibiotics just to fight infection. They repeated this surgical treatment until the wound was infection free. Only then did they begin the permanent reconstruction. Then followed the healing and rehabilitation. It was a long involved and painful process. I could visualize the analogy of this process in me. All that removing and cleaning and packing, repeat – I saw all those years of learning and growing before we* *moved to Arizona. I thought of the times I had felt overwhelmed by information. It was more than I could process – too much too fast. I felt like a canary getting a drink from a fire hose. The flushing of the wound in the microsurgery prep made sense of that. It helped address the negative feelings of why this has taken so long. It wasn't that I had failed to learn, it was preparation for the deeper, more precise work of* **The Pursuer***. The whole process is another major portion of the puzzle.*[26]

I've been through many processes, and now I understand it's a part of life. Because we're alive, we'll go from one process to another. Because living things grow and growth is a continual process.

Give yourself ample grace to own whatever process you need.

OWN THE VICTORY YOU CAN'T SEE: YOU CAN OVERCOME

Now all glory to God, who is able, through his mighty power at work within us, to accomplish infinitely more than we might ask or think.

——Paul

Overcoming. The word itself implies there's a problem. Problems talk to us. They talk like they have all the power; like a bully at school who struts and throws his (or her) weight around. But problems are not all-powerful. It doesn't matter how big they are or how long we've had them. There's a solution. We might not know the solution, yet. If we'll take ownership of the victory we can't see, but believe exists, we move in the direction of our solution.

Some solutions are quick. Some solutions are long and drawn out. Some solutions aren't what we want, or they come about through a way we don't want. Consider Naaman, for example. This guy, in the Bible, had leprosy. He heard he could get healed by a prophet named Elisha. But Naaman had the *how* all figured out in his head, instead of owning the victory. The prophet gave Naaman instructions he didn't like, and he almost went home keeping the disease. Then his servant offered him wisdom. Naaman decided to listen to the wisdom of his servant and do what he didn't want to do—to humble himself and follow directions. Then he got healed.

I find myself repeating a line from my first book, "*I've gotten where I am by refusing to stay where I was.*" It's how I owned the victory I couldn't see but believed existed. I believed victory existed because these two verses in the Bible say God will provide it:

But thanks be to God! He gives us the victory through our Lord Jesus Christ.

But thanks be to God, who always leads us in victory through Christ. God uses us to spread his knowledge everywhere like a sweet-smelling perfume.

I didn't know how God would do it, but I knew He promised, so I dared to believe Him. For example, when I was sick with candidiasis, I wouldn't let go of the belief I could be healed. I got healed by following the leading of the Spirit of Grace. As I look back, I see how He led me through. Also, when my mom had cancer, they gave her three to six months to live. She prayed for, and owned twelve, and I agreed with her. We followed the leading of the Spirit of Grace and she lived fourteen months. Again, as I look back, I can see the process of how He led us both through. When my son separated from our family for reasons I didn't understand at the time, I dared to believe restoration existed. The pain was blinding but I'd come to believe God's faithfulness and His promises are true. It was a long journey where I learned to believe for restoration *right*, not restoration *fast*. I remembered Naaman. The prayer God put in my heart on the journey to victory was, "*as fast as possible but as slow as necessary."* The wait was worth it, and the restoration has been miraculous.

You can own the victory that exists because the Bible promises it to you.

OWN THE BUILDING PROCESS: NEW MINDSETS NEED TO BE BUILT

In order to have a new life, there needs to be new thinking.

—Unknown

Getting new thinking takes work. New thinking means new mindsets, and they must be built. Telling someone to think differently is not enough. Thinking is an activity attached to mental pathways. If you need a new life, you need new mindsets. One might argue mindset—singular. I'm saying mindsets, plural, on purpose. We have more than one. Life is full of topics: family, work, health, friendship, dreams, self-worth, God, life in general, and this list goes on. We have a mindset for every topic. They might be similar, or drastically different. Changing our life means addressing them all.

Let's look at what a mindset is.

- It's preset attitudes that interpret life as we encounter it.
- It's the habitual thought processes preceding our responses.
- It's the program running in our mind that we've downloaded, either by accident or on purpose.
- Simply. It's what we think unconsciously before we act.

You may have a healthy mindset on the topic of work but not when it comes to family. Keep the healthy one, and work on the one you want different. It'll take time and a course of action. It took practice to build an unhealthy mindset, and it'll take a process to build a new one. Remember the power of *instead* in the chapter on *Owning Your Mind*.

By owning your building process, you allow it to take as much time as it needs. Measure by improvement, and celebrate progress. Remind yourself it's a journey. Don't forget to give yourself grace. God has plenty to provide.

Building new mindsets will create a new life.

OWN YOUR INNER DIALOGUE: IT'S REVEALED WHEN YOU SPEAK

A good man brings good things out of the good stored up in his heart, and an evil man brings evil things out of the evil stored up in his heart. For the mouth speaks what the heart is full of.

—Jesus.

One summer my husband and I went to an art fair. While meandering about, I noticed a clock in the square. It had these words on it: *To everything there is a season and a time to every purpose under heaven.* It captivated me and I started taking photographs of it with my phone. My puzzled husband asked me what I was doing, and why. I answered with a short snippet and continued to be absorbed in what I was doing. My answer only puzzled him, so he inquired further. I found myself at a loss for words, and a flood of emotion ensued. I fumbled to give him an explanation, but the emotions clouded my mind. Not my finest hour. It wasn't until the following day I discovered what'd happened. The emotional cloud was a negative inner dialogue of fear and shame. This inner dialogue was so set in my mind I was unconscious of it—until it came out of my mouth with negative words.

This place called the unconscious is a place of power. It feeds the conscious. It's where the mind is *set* through either repetition or trauma.

Minds are busy places. We're always thinking something unless we're actively making ourselves inwardly quiet, which can be quite difficult. This constant thinking is an inner meditation, where we're talking to ourselves. Yes, talking to ourselves. So, what do *you* say when you talk to yourself? Your mouth will tell on you, just like mine told on me at the art fair. The scripture is true that *the mouth speaks what our heart is full of.* Our hearts become full of what we constantly tell ourselves.

There are three ways I found we talk to ourselves with this inner dialogue:

- Negative – Listening to our inner critic, or bully, beating ourselves up. (I was doing this at the art fair.)
- Nice – Telling ourselves we're doing our best, we're only human, and it could be worse. (Helpful but lacking in power.)
- Noble – Honoring our intrinsic value given by God, reminding ourselves there's *no condemnation* because *you're the righteousness of God in Christ* and *God will help you.* This kind of thinking gets built by reading and rehearsing what the Spirit of Grace has to say in the Bible to us. (This one I've found life-changing.)

Where do you find yourself? If you're not sure, listen to how you talk. Your mouth will reveal the truth, and then you know where to begin to build new mindsets.

Inner dialogue, no matter how stubborn, can be changed through process.

OWN YOUR MOUTH: IT HOLDS THE POWER OF CHANGE

Death and life are in the power of the tongue.

—Solomon

Our mouths are powerful in two ways. One, listening to our mouth reveals what's going on inside of us as we talked about. Two, we can use our mouth to change the thing it reveals. The preset habitual thinking running in the background of our mind, our subconscious can be reprogrammed to how we *want* it to talk to us. Everyday life will automatically feed our minds a mixture of good and bad through the things we hear. We can only control some of it. For example, the music we hear at a store, as opposed to what we play in our car. By feeding our mind intentionally, we can get the results we want.

We can overwrite the old mindset with a new mindset using the power of *instead*. Remember the example of technology in the chapter on *Owning Your Mind*. We do this by speaking out loud, so our ears hear our voice saying what we have chosen to believe. This is how I've reprogrammed my mind.

Hearing. I learned I need to hear it. Thinking alone didn't work. Thoughts are weaker than the spoken word. I had to take the fight with my inner dialogue out of my mind, where it played on auto-repeat and put it in my mouth. For example, when I used to suffer terribly with condemnation and confusion, it was due to my negative inner dialogue. Because both condemnation and confusion are rooted in spiritual things, I needed spiritual things to replace them.

Condemnation reduces humans to nothingness. But we're not nothing to God. We're precious to Him. Condemnation came because of sin. Jesus came to deal with the problem of sin *once and for all*. Jesus, the perfect Son of God, laid down His life, and with His blood bought us eternal redemption. That means although we deserved to die because of sin, God considered us worthy to be rescued, because of His love. It amazes me to see how God intercepted us with the power of *instead*. The Bible says *He became sin* and died instead of us. Jesus took the condemnation that belonged to us and gave us the ability to generate His righteousness instead.

Confusion is like a tornado bringing disorder, and *God is not the source of it*. Inner turbulence is stilled by words of peace from the Spirit of Grace. This happens by developing a righteousness mindset. What I mean by a righteousness mindset is viewing ourselves how God does—righteous because of Jesus, instead of condemned because of sin. When our minds are preoccupied with our failings, or sin, our inner dialogue is negative.

God helped me change my inner dialogue by providing alternate words to reprogram my mind. I shared these previously in *Owning Your Mind*. Repeating them is intentional because we learn by repetition, and I want to demonstrate how the mind and mouth work together.

Read the following out loud if you suffer from condemnation and confusion.

- *There is no condemnation for me who is in Christ Jesus.*
- *It is for freedom that Christ has set me free.*
- *The one who is throwing me into confusion will pay the penalty, whoever he may be.*
- *That kind of persuasion does not come from the one who calls me.*
- *But the fruit of the Spirit is love, joy, peace, patience, kindness, goodness, faithfulness, gentleness, and self-control. Against such things there is no law.*

Speaking those words out loud was how I began to overcome the debilitating condemnation and confusion. Change didn't happen overnight. It took time and practice. Each time I spoke those words, in the order given, little by little they demolished the miserable mindset I suffered with and replaced it with a new one. The result was an increasing calm. Once grace was revealed to me—as the all-powerful goodness of God at work on my behalf (instead of a religious term)—condemnation and confusion were defeated, and I became free.

Using words of life from the Spirit of Grace is how I anchored my mind in the truth. Using my mouth to speak words of life, is how I overthrew the old and established the new. It wasn't abracadabra. That would've been easy. This was a laborious re-teaching method using repetition. It took me a lot of time and practice. If you want to employ this procedure, it will take you time, also. You didn't get where you are overnight, so you won't get where you want to be instantly, either. Remember, give yourself grace as you go.

Taking control of your mouth is a skill to govern your thinking.

OWN YOUR PUZZLE PIECES: WE DON'T KNOW EVERYTHING

Now our knowledge is partial and incomplete, and even the gift of prophecy reveals only part of the whole picture!

—Paul

As a child, I asked *why* all the time; so much so, I remember a certain snapshot moment where I frustrated my mother. My mom liked to hang laundry out to dry on what's called a clothesline. We were in the backyard, hanging a load of wet towels. I would grab a towel and attach it to the clothesline with the wooden things called clothespins, but my mom stopped me. She told me first I had to shake out the towel (in a snapping manner, she demonstrated) before attaching it to the clothesline. I dared to ask why, and she snapped, *"why do you always have to ask why?"* I don't remember what I said. Maybe nothing. I just wanted to know. It's part of being human. We want to know.

I don't know everything, and neither do you. Only God knows, and He doesn't always share. He has His reasons. We don't always need to know; or, it's not time because of a situation; or, because we're not ready. Sometimes it's better to not know certain things. Have you ever found out something you wish you could unknow?

I have this story of me doing something dumb to illustrate. Not only did I do something stupid, but I also didn't realize how stupid and unnecessary it was until it was too late. *Duh!* Head slap! No going back in time. My old negative inner dialogue wanted to start, but instead of condemning myself, I saw a lesson in it for me, and you. What dumb thing did I do?

I told my granddaughter something she didn't need to know. She was three years old at the time—the age where kids ask a lot of questions. One of her favorites was *"what's that?"* even when she knew what it was. Answering her question this time, I did it stupidly. We were having a family BBQ and setting up the food line on the counter. There was a big onion on the counter, and she asked her question, *"what's that?"* In my zeal to teach, I told her it was an onion, and then some characteristics about onions. Specifically, I told her when you cut them, they make you cry.

Duh! Head slap! Why?

When her mom asked her if she wanted an onion on her hamburger, she said no, because she didn't want to cry. Clearly, I gave her too much information. She didn't understand. I meant well, but it was information she didn't need.

Likewise, there are times we ask God questions and don't get an answer. When this happens, remember my onion story. Maybe you wouldn't understand at this stage of your life. This is where trust comes in. God is never stupid. He doesn't do dumb things like me. Dumb and stupid are weaknesses of being human. Perhaps that's why He gives us puzzle pieces. These puzzle pieces are little bits of information we need to know to help us and protect us, but they're incomplete.

Life is intricate. We're complex beings. Knowledge often comes to us in pieces. I call them puzzle pieces. Puzzle pieces don't always make sense. Save these tidbits of information. Moments. Revelations. Or however they come. Allow the Spirit of Grace to piece them together as you're ready. He knows you. He knows the picture they make. Own the pieces and your trust in God.

Life is a journey. You can trust the author of life to put your puzzle together. When He gives you a piece, receive it. Let it be all it is, while still being incomplete. Allow the wonder to unfold as He puts your pieces together or elaborates on them. The questions are welcomed. But the "why's" go on forever. Your story is incomplete until it's over.

Own the incompleteness in your puzzle pieces.

OWN YOUR JOURNEY: LIFE IS ERRATIC

Consider it pure joy, my brothers and sisters, whenever you face trials of many kinds, because you know that the testing of your faith produces perseverance. Let perseverance finish its work so that you may be mature and complete, not lacking anything.

—James

Once we become adults, we understand life isn't a bowl of cherries. Things don't always go as planned. Stuff happens. And when things happen, we have a choice on how we're going to proceed.

We can feel sorry for ourselves making ourselves powerless victims, or we can take ownership of our journey.

This meme is true.

The comparison of those can be discouraging and intimidating. But with an adjustment in mindset and attitude, we can rise above. We can own the journey and choose to see it as an adventure. Then, when things don't go as smoothly as we'd like, we see it as part of the adventure. For example, I started an online store called Soul Worthy. It happened rather impulsively. I'd been interested in starting an online store for a while when I was inspired by someone else's experience. This led me to write down a thousand items I could sell in this online store. After I accomplished my list (which was an adventure all its own) I took the inspiring person's free online course. I thought I'd learn about how to open and run a store in this course. However, it was more actionable than I expected. While doing the course I was led through the steps to open the store, bring in products and run it. I had an online store operational in six days. That's fantastic if you have the passion, focus and time to dedicate to it. At first, I thought I did. After three months it became clear, I didn't. Although I found it fun and a great outlet for my creativity, it needed more time and attention than I had to give. I had my epiphany while going through the rewrites on this section of this book. I needed to do what I was writing—take ownership of my journey. I needed to shut down the store because it wasn't going as planned. It had become a drain and distraction. It was a difficult decision to make because I'd gotten emotionally attached to it. To help me through this change I ordered two things as souvenirs to remember it as an adventure instead of a failure.

When things don't go as planned, the Spirit of Grace helps me and encourages me. I believe He'll find a way to bring good out of it. Like a child brings a broken toy to a loving parent, I can bring my broken plans, or dreams to Him. He'll comfort me and provide a new plan.

Life is erratic, but we can live it fully, and enjoy the journey. Imagine a roller coaster, surfing, skiing, or any other form of entertainment or sports, that has ups and downs. When we have *the greater One in us,* and with us, on our journey, we can enjoy. We can learn. We can prevail.

Take ownership of your journey, and you'll have more joy.

OWN THE POWER OF *INSTEAD*

Instead, let the Spirit renew your thoughts and attitudes.

—Paul

In the chapter on *Owning Your Mind,* I explained what the power of *instead* is, and an example of it in my life. In a previous section, we talked about owning your mouth, and how it works with the mind. *Instead,* words work because when you use them, you employ the power of faith. You don't need to have giant faith. A little is enough when it's real. Jesus said, faith as small as *"a grain of mustard seed"* was enough to move the mountains in our lives. But sometimes we forget what He said our faith does: it comes out of our mouth when our heart is full of it. Faith speaks. *Instead,* words are spoken out loud.

When you're going through something hard, or know you will, you can prepare *instead* words, and speak them out in faith. I did this after an incident occurred that triggered me back to first-grade. As I wrote in *Owning Your Mess,* I had to own the truth and call it trauma. As I wrote in *Owning Your Mind,* I had to own the negative mindset created by the trauma. My victory over the flashbacks and repeated emotional breakdowns came through the practice of employing *instead* words, as led by the Spirit of Grace. I needed something to instantaneously stop the dark abyss of emotional despair from consuming me. I felt like what I wanted was a fantasy, like a *silver bullet* is said to stop a werewolf. But I believed God was real and would help me.

I called the *instead* words I used to overcome a *silver bullet*. A *silver bullet* is a specific short verbal response to say *instead* of what the emotions, or fear, wanted me to say. The *silver bullet* confronted and corrected the negative inner dialogue playing in the unconscious part of my mind. To find my *silver bullet,* I needed to identify the root of my problem. God showed me it was a lie I believed about my value. Through the process of prayer, and the leading of the Spirit of Grace, the silver bullet forged was this: *I Matter!* I started speaking it daily over and over. It sounded silly, but I knew I needed it like medicine. I'd say it in the face of debilitating emotional pain—sometimes with tears running down my face. But I'd say it, over and over until it became a part of me, because the *silver bullet* was the truth, and the truth will win over lies every time. I matter, and so do you!

Internalizing the truth, instead of lies, will change how you live.

OWN YOUR VALIDATION PROCESS: TRAUMA IS PERSONAL

Scars have voices, and secrets are not silent. These need to be resolved for us to be truly free. The simple "get over it," "just stop that," or "it isn't that bad," are insufficient. There needs to be validation and process to heal.

—Danielle Bernock

You will never heal of trauma without acknowledging its presence. That's what validation is. I failed to heal of childhood traumas because I diminished them. I dismissed their existence; but, it didn't dismiss them from my life. They went underground. What has happened has happened and cannot unhappen. Time machines don't exist. To resolve traumas, they must be validated, acknowledged, taken out of the dark, and brought into the light.

It doesn't matter how big, or little, they look to others. Trauma is personal. If it traumatized you, it traumatized you. There's a wound, and there's a reason. There may be many multiple wounds, and therefore many reasons. These reasons have a cause. Someone is traumatized—Because.

Because is a powerful part of validation. I learned this in a two-part process from a song by Kelly Clarkson with the help from the Spirit of Grace. I touched on it briefly in *Owning Your Mess,* but there's more to it.

Part one: Blame

The song by Kelly *Because of You* is about the effects of childhood trauma. It reveals the side-effects of fear, inner vows to self-protect, emotional hiding, and shame. It's a cry of anguish, pointing the finger of blame at the one who caused it. I knew the same soul-crushing pain but never imagined the blame outside of myself before. I'd always blamed myself. It's what children do. But self-blame invalidates the trauma and traps the child in a prison of pain.

This song revealed to me, I wasn't to blame for the trauma in my childhood; *because,* someone else was. It took the blame from inside of me, where the pain lived, and assigned it to another. I can't say it enough. Children are NOT to blame for their trauma.

Part two: Cause

In my journey, some of the people who hurt me were malicious, and some were not. I tripped over the non-malicious ones. I couldn't assign blame because they didn't intend to hurt me. When the Spirit of Grace separated the human, *who* was guilty of hurting me, from *what* they did, He changed the focus to how it had affected my soul.

- Because.
- There was a cause.
- There was an effect.

Healing came into view as blame transformed into the cause, instead of judgment. Judgment and blame became useless *because* the past can't be changed. It happened and can't un-happen. The cause can't be removed, but the effect can be healed. Blame had a place in the process. But focusing on it would've trapped me in the pain.

It doesn't matter where the blame is put. It'll become toxic if held onto like a teddy bear. The *teddy bear,* named Blame, will bite the one holding it. It's better to identify the cause and tend to the effect—the wound. Choose to heal. Let go of blame and allow the Spirit of Grace to help you own your healing.

Dealing with the cause and effect validates your trauma so you can move into healing.

OWN YOUR HEALING PROCESS: DISCOVER A NEW YOU

Some people are afraid of what they might find if they try to analyze themselves too much. But you have to crawl into your wounds to discover where your fears are. Once the bleeding starts, the cleansing can begin.

—Tori Amos

Being healed of your trauma won't eradicate all your memories. What it'll do is eliminate their power over you. Remember, it'll be a process. It'll take time and a lot of courageous work. But *because you matter*, you owe it to yourself to take ownership of your life by owning your wholeness through healing. Freedom is possible.

You heal the wound by tending to the effect, instead of focusing on the cause. Looking at and tending to soul wounds, apart from the person, or the incident, is how you tend to the effect. This is where healing happens. For example, if someone gets pushed off a building and breaks a leg, where does the focus need to be? On the building? The ground they landed on? The person who pushed them off the building? Whether it was intentional or an accident? No. No. No. To heal, the immediate focus must be on the broken bone—the wound. The broken bone requires certain actions, not only to heal but to heal properly. The bone must be set properly. It must be held in place by a cast and given time to heal. The pain must be comforted; and when the cast is removed, there will still be more recovery. Remember the newly emerged butterfly's need for a new process. Healing is a process.

Somehow this is obvious to us when it's our physical bodies. Our souls deserve the same loving care and attention we give to our bodies.

The Spirit of Grace led me not only to freedom and healing but to a thriving I didn't know existed before my journey. It was also *because,* like the section above—cause and effect. But this *cause and effect* was all because of God, and it was good, instead of bad. I spend time every morning with the Spirit of Grace. One morning, as I was reading words in the Bible I read every day, I saw it. No, I heard it, because the words escaped my mouth, revealing to myself what was in my heart, as we talked about earlier. After I read the portion of scripture, I heard myself say *all because of you* to the Spirit of Grace. When I did, I saw a different source as the *you,* in *Because of You,* than I had when validating my trauma. This validated the blessings in my life and their source as the Spirit of Grace. I was reading: *But blessed is the man who trusts in the Lord and has made the Lord his hope and confidence. He is like a tree planted along a riverbank, with its roots reaching deep into the water—a tree not bothered by the heat nor worried by long months of drought. Its leaves stay green, and it goes right on producing all its luscious fruit.* All because of Him.

All the pain I'd known was because of the failings of people. All the healing and good in my life is because of the Spirit of Grace. Both are causative. Now when I hear those three words, *Because of You*, I think of my God who is love, loves me, and who healed my soul. I think of all He's done in my life, and all I have, because of Him.

Facing the truth, and peeling back the curtain of your soul, to discover what's beneath, can be scary and painful; but, it's the only way to healing. It's your life. It's your choice. It's your trauma. It takes courage. No one else needs to understand. Only you do. Become a new you by seeing a new you, and let love heal your soul.

Owning your healing process is the doorway to wholeness, and the true you.

KEY POINTS

- No two journeys through any process will be identical even if we take the same steps.
- Problems are not all-powerful. There's a solution.
- Building new mindsets will create a new life.
- Inner dialogue, no matter how stubborn, can be changed through process.
- Taking control of your mouth is a skill to govern your thinking.
- Life is intricate. Knowledge often comes to us in puzzle pieces.
- With an adjustment in mindset and attitude, we can choose to see our life as an adventure.
- Dealing with the cause and effect validates your trauma so you can move into healing.
- Owning your healing process is the doorway to wholeness, and the true you.

YOU CAN ASK GOD FOR HELP

Spirit of Grace, show me what processes I need. Help me trust them because you love me. Hear the questions in my soul and tell me what I need to know, even if it's a puzzle piece.

NOTES

How Naomi Took Ownership Of Her Life

Because anything can happen at any time, I want to be sure that whatever I leave behind is gonna be positive and lifting up to someone else.

—Naomi Trotto

I've known Naomi her entire life. Choosing to interview her for this book was a no-brainer. I've watched her take ownership of her life long before I knew how to take ownership of my own. In fact, she has helped me on my journey. She's a strong and courageous woman who stared death in the face, overcame PTSD, and is owning the path to obtain her dreams.

It was through taking ownership that Naomi entered her current career. As a child she used to wake up with braids in her hair; evidently braiding it herself while sleeping. Doing hair was something that came easily to her; but she had no interest in being a hairdresser. The industry as she knew it, was stigmatized as a side hustle for stay at home moms. Naomi was more interested in business and having a career. She secured various manager positions and had a company car until she could stand it no longer. "*Being a hairdresser was something chasing me. I feel God gave me a skill set, and I have to use it. I don't exactly know what all I will be doing with that skill set and with the knowledge I have, but it chased me and so I had to make a lot of sacrifices in order to go to beauty school at all.*" In 2005 she left her job to attend David Pressley School of Cosmetology.

Naomi's school participated in an event called *The Real Big Hairball* in Royal Oak, Michigan. "*It's an artistic expression of art* utilizing hair and wardrobe. That was where I did my first braided Mohawk." The hair in this show was nothing a person would wear every day. It's crazy *"off the wall, something that is an artist scheme, something that is open to interpretation."* This kind of hair is called avant garde. Naomi took ownership of her passion for it, and herself as a hair artist.

Birthed within her was a dream to *"do hair for films, for directors such as Tim Burton or the people who did "the Hunger Games." Things that are a little bit out there. When you're watching them, you're like, 'why is the hair like that?' That's what I'm good at. And that's where I live."*

But on her way to obtain her dreams, trauma reared its ugly head. Naomi was slow to own becoming a mom, due to stigmas she wrestled with and the dreams in her heart. She and her husband were married for four years before they chose to become parents. Being pregnant was difficult enough for Naomi *"but then he ended up coming early and I lived a decent amount of time believing that that was my fault."* The first time she held her son was hours after he was born. The self-condemnation was loud and paralyzing. In the NICU she whispered an apology to him with tears streaming down her face. While her insides screamed *"Okay, well, I suck at life, so, the end,"* she plodded along trying to not feel so horrible. For nine years Naomi participated in the March of Dimes Walk for Babies as penance because she blamed herself.

An opportunity came Naomi's way soon after. *"The film industry came to Michigan for a very short time. During that time, I was able to be an extra in The Citizen multiple times, for multiple days in a row."* Taking this opportunity put her in the backstage film environment. It allowed her to see if reality and her dreams met. She loved it. There was a hair trailer on set, and she inquired how a person gets in there. The producer's assistant only gave her two words—be relevant. Motivated by those words Naomi decided to create a bridal team. It was just the beginning of big things to come.

It took four years, and the heart desire of her son for a sibling, before Naomi would own motherhood again. This time it almost killed her. Literally.

Determined to succeed she *"did everything right. I mean, literally everything by the book, everything I was supposed to do. I did everything that they told me to do."* But doing everything right didn't make for success. Naomi developed complications in her already high-risk pregnancy.

Not due until September, in June Naomi began to swell and her blood pressure started rising. Over the fourth of July weekend she had orders to collect her urine for the doctor to test. Diagnosed with pre-eclampsia her doctor sent her to the hospital to be monitored and put on a magnesium drip for an incapacitating headache. But pre-eclampsia turned into the very rare HELLP syndrome (hemolysis, elevated liver enzymes, low platelet count). *"Basically, the gist of it is your liver and kidneys stop working, and your body to its entirety shuts down completely. The only cure for it is to remove the child. So, delivering my daughter was more of a removal of the disease than a beautiful situation. That was incredibly intense and incredibly traumatic because I mean, for obvious reasons."* Here she and her husband had a stare-down with death and took ownership of hope. As they took Naomi to the operating room her family sat in the waiting room praying.

Naomi found herself alive but in the same situation of blaming herself for her daughter's premature birth. It was heartbreaking that other family members were able to see her daughter before she could. But when she did, Naomi whispered the same apology she had given to her son. It was three days before she could hold her. While her daughter lived in the NICU for over a month, Naomi was there every day.

Although Naomi almost died, her dreams still danced within her but there were some serious things in the way. *"After I had Mia I started in therapy. I realized that I had some PTSD, I had some postpartum depression, and a bunch of things I had not dealt with before."* Naomi began the hard work with her counselor. One of the first things she learned that helped her move forward was, *"I can't control many things in life, and that I have to control how I handle them, as opposed to trying to control the life around me."*

Two years later, Naomi took ownership of another step toward her dream and Bell Amore Salon was born. *"As far as being an owner, it was never a dream of mine to own a salon. It was more of an understanding that that would be part of the process."* As expected, being a salon owner opened up opportunities for Naomi. She was sought out by a non-profit called *A Beautiful Me* that helps young girls take ownership of their value. They wanted Naomi and her staff to participate in their annual avant garde hair show. Naomi and her assistant participated and took first place. *"It was an interesting experience, because I had to make everything in advance and then put my work out there for people to judge it in front of my face."*

Having her work in print was becoming common for Naomi. She was doing photo shoots, entering contests, building her social media profile and the bridal team was doing quite well. Looking for other opportunities to set herself apart she found out about an elite group called the Unicorn Tribe. Naomi wanted into this group. *"I looked into what I needed to do, looked into what they were looking for, and then set my sights on achieving it."* She did many models for free and worked to improve her color skills.

A client and friend helped her attain her goal. Eddie started coming to Naomi he was sixteen. *"He came every two weeks for me to cut his hair and he was openly gay. I was the first person who he came out to and he would show up to fundraisers and stuff for March for babies. We had a really great relationship."* Something Naomi wanted to do for her goal of being accepted on the Unicorn Tribe was *"do a men's haircut with a rainbow color."* At that time Eddie was working as a receptionist at the salon. She did the rainbow on Eddie and it turned out stunning. After many photos she returned his hair to its natural color for his new job he was starting at Gucci.

Naomi was inducted into the Unicorn Tribe and Eddie was starting the path to his dream job. Exciting things were on the horizon. But Naomi never got to tell him her accomplishment. A phone call delivered horrific news—Eddie's dead. How could that be? He was just in her chair yesterday. *"That rocked my world quite a bit, because I'd never had anyone that physically close to me that had died tragically, all of a sudden, like that. And so that became a very large traumatic point for me. I had to work through that in a million different ways."*

Dark grief overshadowed Naomi and she wanted to stay in bed all day being depressed. But when she thought about her team at the salon dealing with their grief, her kids and husband at home who needed her, a career she was building; she told herself *"no, you don't get an option of hiding."* She had to figure out a way to deal with this and move forward. Knowing Eddie wouldn't be happy with her hiding motivated her. Naomi got a tattoo of her scissors, started doing yoga, reached out for help to trusted friends to talk it through. She struggled to make sense of it. *"He was gone. And he didn't get to do the things he was doing. And I literally had talked to him the day before. He was in my chair the day before. I was in denial for a long time. He was a positive influence on everyone that he met. And anyone who knew him would say that."*

Naomi is a big believer in taking ownership. But she understands a person needs to see something to own it. When her daughter was born premature, she started to see how it wasn't her fault *"because there was no way that I could have prevented that."* Processing that helped her turn her self-punishment from her son's birth into grief work. Nine years later she and her husband realized that doing the yearly walk was no longer needed. It served its purpose. When she learned the professionals doing hair for films are in their fifties and sixties, she owned patience and made a long-term goal.

I asked Naomi where she got her all her strength and courage from. Her reply was long. She talked about how she was raised and never doubted her value, had a strong foundation in her faith, and then listed person after person and relationship after relationship that helped her become who she is today.

Naomi calls her husband *"the most supportive human on the planet."* She knows without a doubt that when her opportunity comes to fulfill her dream, he'll do whatever is necessary for her to follow through. Not many women I know can say that. And then there's her best friend she met in college. *"She is the one female relationship that's always had an authenticity and a good reality to it that is different from anything else that I've ever experienced ever before. I need that."*

Helping each of her staff take ownership of their journey is important to Naomi. She's not just their boss, they're building dreams together. And behind the chair she helps others take ownership of their lives also. *"In what I do for a living being a hairdresser people want to tell me all their problems. I'm very solution minded, inherently trying to find a solution to the problem. And I'm able to use my experiences, my therapy, and my ownership of the different things that I've done. I try to pass that on to other people every single day."*

Find out more about Naomi and what she has to offer in
the endnotes.

CHAPTER 12

Owning Your Wholeness

I am a human. I can only be loved into wholeness.

—Unknown

HOW TO BEGIN

What I mean when I say wholeness is the feeling of completeness, soundness, security: spirit, soul, and body. I became whole through my relationship with the Spirit of Grace. Because of that, I talk about Him and the things He's shown me a lot in this chapter. Becoming whole takes place both in an instant and over the entire course of our lives. The promise of wholeness and the position of wholeness was mine the moment I connected with the one who created me. The connection made me complete in one aspect. But in the emotional, mental, and experiential aspect, I am becoming more and more whole. Both required knowing love.

I dare you to be loved into wholeness.

OWN YOUR FREEDOM TO DISCOVER AND KNOW GOD

Now this is eternal life: that they know you, the only true God, and Jesus Christ, whom you have sent.

—Jesus

As children, we all have dreams and wishes. I always wished I could fly. In my dreams, while sleeping I'd often be flying. I never had wings, yet I could fly. Wings symbolize flying. Flying symbolizes freedom to me.

We were created to be free. Yet more often than not, we find ourselves bound by one thing or another. I believe the greatest freedom we were created for, is to know God and enjoy His presence. Legalism balks at that. Legalism says we were created for the sole purpose of serving God and obeying Him. That's wrong. I say we're created to know and enjoy Him. The gospel is not a summons to work or to be a slave. It's an invitation to reconnect with God and rest in His work. Everything we need, He's provided. It's an invitation to come to Him. It's so simple, it gets messed up by people who fail to understand. It's not complicated, and once we *get it,* we're so elated inside, we soar; or, as I put it in my first book, we get wings. And getting them is just the beginning of a wonderful adventure. The adventure of exploring who God is and all He's done, our relationship with Him and others, is a lifelong adventure. Stephen Curtis Chapman wrote a song a long time ago: *The Great Adventure.* I didn't *get it* then. I was still bound by lies, wrong thinking, and works mentality with a *God loves you, but . . .* way of thinking. But Stephen had it right: *The love of God will take us far beyond our wildest dreams.* God wants us to be as joyful as little kids and explore. It's as simple as letting Him be God and recognizing we're not. It takes humility. Pride wants God's job. I don't.

Being independent and autonomous sounds noble. However, living in interdependence is a much richer way to live. We need relationships. Living in connection with others satisfies a deep place in our souls. There's a reason solitary confinement is a punishment. It's the same with God. To know Him is to live interdependent[27] with Him. Can a beautiful rose live and give its beauty to the world without the plant in which it grows? It can't. Likewise, I believe we can't become the fullness of who we are, without interdependence with our creator. God has arms open wide. Take Him up on His offer, and soar, and explore. You'll never be the same.

Own your freedom to explore knowing God.

OWN THE MYSTERY: SUPERNATURAL THINGS HAPPEN

The wind blows wherever it pleases. You hear its sound, but you cannot tell where it comes from or where it is going. So it is with everyone born of the Spirit.

—Jesus

The things we see, feel, taste, and touch, are part of our natural world. They're very real to us. Sometimes we can feel like that's all there is, but there's more. Supernatural things happen. I'm not going to go off on some creepy thing here. Supernatural means above the natural. It's outside the realm of where we see, feel, taste, and touch. It's a place we don't understand. It's a mystery.

There are things we know; but, there are more things we don't. We don't have to understand the things we don't know to partake of the benefits of their mystery. For example, we plant a garden and enjoy the harvest. We understand part of the process, but there are laws of life at work we don't fully understand or control. For instance, *how* does dirt make a seed sprout and grow? *How* does something so small produce such abundance? We can't explain it fully. It's a mystery. So are things of the spirit, or supernatural. It takes faith to plant a seed, believing it will grow. It takes faith in God and His word, to believe we can have what He says. The Spirit of Grace operates in ways that are often mysterious. When we own the mystery, we're exhibiting faith.

I've experienced this repeatedly. You have too, even if you haven't noticed. A favorite example of mine is when I wrote music to a song when I was beginning to see a young man. The same night, he wrote a poem. He shared it with me, and the two went together. It was a mystery that spoke to me. I embraced it and more mysteries followed. These mysteries led to the young man becoming my husband. Another mystery occurred when my daughter-in-law was pregnant living in Texas—away from us in Arizona. She planned on having a natural, home birth. Scheduling to be there wasn't possible. Babies don't arrive on cue. She passed her due date and was going to be permitted to go two more weeks, before inducing. We were waiting on the unknown. One day I felt I had to go. Just inside. No natural evidence. If I went on what I was *feeling*, using the time off work I had available, and she went the whole two weeks without birthing, I'd miss it. Yet inside, I felt a nudge. I went. I was there for the birth. A mystery. Someone might dismiss the mysteries as coincidence. I do not.

Owning the mystery is a wonder-filled thing.

OWN YOUR SPIRITUAL LIFE INSTEAD OF RELIGION

It is the Spirit who gives life; the flesh is no help at all. The words that I have spoken to you are spirit and life.

—Jesus

Religion is a strange word. It's used both in the positive and negative. I dislike the word because it's misused as a description. To me, the word religion is oppressive. It's man manipulating God . . . or trying to. Oppressive religion is all about what a person must do.

Rules to be followed. An angry God to appease. A pecking order to adhere to. This kind of religion hurt me deeply. It put me on display, as not good enough, as a child. It was deeply humiliating and shaming. It destroyed my sense of value. Not only in my own eyes, but also in how I believed God saw me. Religion made an example of me. Oppressive religion said *try harder*. I despise this kind of religion the more I understand it.

It was through taking ownership of my own spiritual life, freedom became visible. I had to reclaim my life from *them*. Whoever *them* was each time. It was quite an involved process. Destructive religion left scars in me that needed healing.

Oppressive religion is like an abusive husband, making promises for what you want, but never delivering. The Bible itself says[28] to throw that kind of religion away. The old covenant of laws that makes us slaves. Instead, we can embrace the freedom God provides by grace through Jesus.

Destructive religion says we're bad apart from God. Jesus says we're incomplete apart from Him. That's a different mindset. In my *"journey to emerge,"* I came to the revelation of *I am we*. This revelation has become ingrained in me since. I find it profound. I, all by myself, am not enough because I'm incomplete. I, all by myself, am lonely. I, all by myself, am weak. But because I matter, God doesn't leave me all by myself. *For God so loved . . .* me . . . you. He desires relationship, union, and oneness. He is our completer. Where religion says we can *never* be good enough, Jesus says joined to me you're enough. In fact, He provides *more than enough*. Together, we are content in relational interaction, because we were designed to be interdependent. Together, we're strong, and whole, because *the person who is joined to the Lord is one spirit with Him*—I am we.

Interdependence with Jesus makes me feel completely whole.

OWN WHAT YOU BELIEVE: YOUR FAITH IS YOURS

... these are written, that ye might believe that Jesus is the Christ, the Son of God; and that believing ye might have life through his name.

—John

Some people say you can't help what you believe. They delegate their faith to their experience, as a cause and effect sort of thing. I used to be like that until I learned faith is a choice I make. What you believe is your choice. It's true that what we experience affects us. But it's not the end of the story. God made us more powerful than our environment, our past, and our experience. What is it you believe?

Sometimes we want to believe, but it's difficult. That's when we owe it to ourselves to dare to believe, like this guy in the Bible, named Abraham. He dared to believe what God told him. God told him he was going to have a son, but he was old, and his wife was not only old but barren, too. It was hard to believe, but he dared to. He started with choosing to believe, hoping it was true. The Bible says it was *in hope that he believed*. It's where we get hoping against hope. It took Abraham a while to become—how the Bible puts it—*fully persuaded*. It took me a long time too. I'm comforted by the story of Abraham. God repeated his promise to Abraham seven times over many years. Each time He gave Abraham *assurance of what Abraham was hoping, making him more certain of his faith*. God even used the power of *instead* to help Abraham believe. He did this by changing Abraham's name. Instead of Abram, he became Abraham, which means father of many. This also helped Abraham by causing him to speak his faith—because of what his new name meant—and his *ears to hear the promise of God, which is how we get faith*.

Getting from wanting to believe, to completely believing, took Abraham years. God was never angry with Abraham along his faith journey. Not even when Abraham's weakness in faith became evident by trying to make God's promise happen himself. Abraham had sex with his wife's handmaid Hagar resulting in a son. It was his wife, Sarah's idea, but he followed along. The whole situation created all kinds of other problems, but let's not get off topic. It was after this incident, God changed Abraham's name. God helps us when we want to believe but we're struggling.

When we struggle to believe, we discover what we really believe by our actions and/or reactions. What's in our heart comes out when we're put under pressure. For instance, if you stepped on a grape, you'd get grape mush. You wouldn't get cherries. It doesn't matter if you want cherries. You have a grape. It's like that in our lives. If we're not getting what we want in life, we need to change what we believe. Like in the illustration of the cherry and grape, you'd need to become a cherry. How is this done? By owning what you believe.

Choosing what you believe is a birthright. The enemy of our soul shrouds the truth in darkness like a magician doing illusions. As light is more powerful than darkness, Jesus is more powerful than the enemy. I've chosen to believe this. It's your choice to believe Jesus is more powerful, or not. What do you want? It is up to you. It's your faith alone. You're empowered when you own it. Then you can put it somewhere, on purpose, when circumstances try to run your life.

Choosing what you believe is taking ownership of your faith, by choice.

OWN WHO YOU REALLY ARE: DARE TO BELIEVE IT

See what great love the Father has lavished on us, that we should be called children of God! And that is what we are!

—John

We weren't designed to be disconnected from God. We were designed to need Him. I believe this separation—or independence—from our creator caused trauma to our souls, resulting in confusion, condemnation, and loss of wholeness. This is referred to in the Bible as *the fall*. I call it the original trauma.

This original trauma happened because a lie was believed, and a bad choice followed. God wasn't surprised by this. Since the beginning, He had a plan to redeem us and restore us to wholeness. Restore us to who He made us to be in the first place—created *a little lower than Himself crowned with glory*. Many translations say angels, but the original Hebrew[29] is *Elohim*, which means God. The lie was that God was holding out on Adam and Eve, so they tried to get what they already had—to be like God. Instead, they lost what they had, and every human born is spiritually traumatized, suffering separation anxiety until they reconnect. Jesus is the fulfillment of God's plan.

If that's difficult to grasp, I have an illustration for you that helped me.

The word "see" came into play. I began hearing about how God sees us and how we need to see how He sees. But then even just getting a look at or learning what He sees isn't enough. The word picture was presented using the movie The Princess Diaries and how she was a princess before she knew she was. How even after she heard she was a princess, she couldn't accept it. And even after she decided to believe the queen she still couldn't "see" herself as one. The movie laid out a very nice word picture of the process and the emotion and the struggle to believe what was a fact but felt so odd, so untrue. Believing in the heart takes time, takes convincing. She was always a princess but she did not always believe it. It wasn't until after she could bring herself to actually believe it and see herself as a princess, that she could partake of the things that went with it and make choices within that context.

It is like that with us. I know I have heard many wonderful things over the years about how God sees me and loves me. Sadly my perceptions of how I saw Him and how I saw myself clouded my view and therefore robbed me of what was mine. Even how I saw others got in the way. The childhood broken mirrors of parents, teachers, peers, religious leaders and bad experiences impaired my ability to see and understand. **The Pursuer** *has a perfect mirror. It is gazing at Jesus, who He is and what all that means. Yet when we look into this mirror we see such a perfection and a LOVE that is difficult to process because it looks too good to be true. Yet it is true so we have to learn to accept it. It is learning to see ourselves how He sees us. We belong to Him. He laid down His life, on purpose, intentionally, because He loves us. It is His desire for us to have the advantage in life. Because of Him we have been given the right to receive help from God. Our hearts argue with such wonderfulness.*[30]

Reconciliation was just the beginning of the plan of Grace. In Romans chapter five the words *much more* are repeated five times. Five times! Jesus restored us *much more* than we lost.

Owning who God says you are opens you up to all He has for you.

OWN THE GLORY THAT CAN BELONG TO YOU

For you know that it was not with perishable things such as silver or gold that you were redeemed from the empty way of life handed down to you from your ancestors, but with the precious blood of Christ, a lamb without blemish or defect.

—Peter

Glory. What does the word mean to you? For a long time, I thought it was wrong to have it. When I was told *all have sinned, and come short of the glory of God*, I had this mental image: *slap your hand if you dare reach for any value.* I thought my wanting to have any value was connected to sin, and pride because it belonged to God alone. I was wrong.

The truth of who God made humans, in the original creation was difficult for me to fathom. We fell so far. The fall, or our traumatizing separation from God, stripped us not only of our glory but also the ability to see the glory. There's a glory belonging to God alone, but there's a glory belonging to us.

We have value in the eyes of God. Jesus shed His precious blood to secure a position for us in Him if we want it. Jesus himself prayed for us. He tells the Father He has given us glory. And not just any glory. See for yourself.

*"I gave them **the same glory you gave me**, so that they may be one, just as you and I are one."* (emphasis mine)

And that wasn't just for the twelve guys he had following Him. Here it is in context, identifying anyone who wants it, and the reason to have it. *"I pray **not only for them**, but **also for those who believe in me** because of their message. I pray that they may **all** be one. Father! May they be in us, just as you are in me and I am in you. May they be one, **so that the world will believe** that you sent me. I gave them **the same glory you gave me,** so that they may be*

***one**, just as you and I are one: I in them and you in me, so that they may **be completely one**, in order **that the world may know that you sent me and that you love them as you love me."** (emphasis mine)

As I see it, the purpose of the glory Jesus gives is for shining the light of unity and love. That's where my glory is found—in my union with God, knowing His love. My union is made possible because of Jesus. His life. His death. His blood. His resurrection. He removed my sin and made me *the righteousness of God* through union. Wow! What a miracle.

Believing Jesus and receiving what He did for us, is how anyone accepts the position He offers. What is this position? Jesus spoke of a kingdom. *A glorious kingdom where we are called royal.* Royal. I'm a commoner as far as the earth goes, so it's hard for me to imagine. I need the story I shared with you about the princess, to help me see this position Jesus authorized for me.

Jesus established *a new covenant, based on better promises* than the old covenant of law, too. In this new covenant, *His ministry is superior* to the guys who were in charge of the old one. Jesus took us from rules-based living to grace-based faith.

This amazing position in His kingdom is offered to us if we want it. We were created for glory. It's our destiny by design, but God won't force it on us.

Shining the glorious light of unity and love is part of our wholeness.

OWN YOUR COMFORT: LONELINESS HAS A CURE

I will not leave you comfortless: I will come to you.

—Jesus

I can only imagine there may be people angry with me for daring to say there's a cure for loneliness. I believe it's true. Even when I fall into the feeling myself. I need this cure also.

I've suffered horrible loneliness. And the cure I say exists, isn't easy to implement all the time. I've struggled with following my own advice. I need to remember in my struggle, I have a choice. I can choose to condemn myself for feeling lonely and finding it hard to not be, or I can see where I am and remind myself how to come out of the loneliness. This is where I first came to this conclusion.

I believe lonely has a cure. You can't order it online. You can't take a pill. You can't will it away. It abides until it ceases to be, ceases to be alone. I believe this is one reason why sharing is so important. But even after sharing with someone else we go back to our alone-ness. This need reveals why it is important that someone is with us even if they can't change negative circumstances going on. Lonely is a horrible feeling. It can be felt in varying degrees. When I picture deep loneliness I see inconsolable sorrow and wailing. It made me think of hell. Hell is something people don't like to talk about. I know I don't. The way I have perceived it in the past was a punishment that I needed to do stuff to avoid. Could it possibly be loneliness is hell? It is our choice of disconnection? The only way I believe this thing called lonely leaves our lives is through knowing **The Pursuer** *is with us. Not just knowing like information, but that "being convinced" kind of knowing. Then you know you are not alone, ever, even if it feels like it, you know better. Comforted instead of lonely.*[31]

I'm not saying you'll never feel lonely again. The cure I speak of is for overcoming, instead of wallowing. I've wallowed. I understand the magnetic pull to wallow in the sorrow of loneliness. It's like a drug. But we can break free from the addiction. This begins with owning your comfort. It's a process. Think of a child learning to self-soothe. Who's in charge of you? Your feelings? Your decisions? You.

It takes courage to own your comfort. It starts with believing it exists. Comfort exists because you're not alone. God has sent His Spirit of Grace to be with you, always. He's also known as the Comfort-er. Loneliness is an emotional detachment. Owning your comfort is embracing attachment. I realize there are times we need comfort in human form. This is still a choice. Choosing connection. Sometimes we balk at this because we don't want to own it. We want others to reach out. To notice. And it's nice when they do. But we don't control others. If we allow our happiness and comfort to be subject to others, we give up our lives to them.

When loneliness shows up, slam the door in its face, by owning your comfort.

KEY POINTS

- Wholeness is the feeling of completeness, soundness, security: spirit, soul, and body.
- God wants us to be as joyful as little kids and explore our relationship with Him.
- The Spirit of Grace operates in ways that are often mysterious.
- Interdependence with Jesus will make you feel completely whole.
- Choosing what you believe is taking ownership of your faith by choice.
- Owning who God says you are, opens you up to all He has for you.
- Shining the glorious light of unity and love is part of our wholeness.
- When loneliness shows up, slam the door in its face by owning your comfort.

YOU CAN ASK GOD FOR HELP

Wow God. I'm amazed at how much you love me, and all you've done for me. Thank you, Jesus. Help me to see and dare to believe so I can enjoy being loved into wholeness by you.

NOTES

How Jeff Took Ownership Of His Life

We are who we are, and we are beautiful and one of a kind.

—Jeff Cavataio

Jeff and I met at an assisted living place where my mother-in-law lived. He was in a rock and roll band but performed at various senior living places on the side. It was the year I published my first book and he was working on his album *Winds of Emotion*. We connected as artists. He shared with me some of the songs he was writing, and I gave him a copy of my book. I admired the sense of honor and respect he carried. It wasn't until my interview with him I understood how many things he's taken ownership of, to be where he is today.

The rock and roll band Jeff played in was quite successful. But that world was wreaking havoc in his life. *"With that level of success there was sex, drugs, and alcohol. It took over my life. I never did any drugs, but I had a major problem with alcohol and women."* One of the women, Aimee, became pregnant. Unlike many young men who sleep around, Jeff took ownership of being the father. *"From the day that she said that she was pregnant we tried to stay together, and we became a couple."* Jeff was there through Aimee's pregnancy. They lived together in a single room at Aimee's aunt's house along with Aimee's three-year-old daughter. He adored his son Landon, and poured himself into the role. To provide for them he drove extreme distances for work, some out of state. *"I was there every step of the way. We tried to do the relationship thing, but it didn't work out."*

As I listened to Jeff unpack this story for me, I heard a young man whose parents raised him to understand the value of that little baby. To appreciate the need to love and be loved. From my first meeting with Jeff I knew how much he loved, honored, and respected his parents. He talked about them all the time. The year I met Jeff he almost lost his mom. He shared the story with me back then and again in my interview. It tore him up and challenged everything he believed. "*My mom is my everything. She is my best friend. She is my rock; she is everything to me.*" His respect for them goes so far that he sat them down the night before our interview, to let them know ugly details they hadn't known before. Like always, they supported him. I was surprised to learn he was adopted.

Jeff hesitated to talk about being adopted because of how much he loves his parents. He fully owns being adopted. I was so glad he decided to share his wonderful adoption story. Jeff was born to a sixteen-year-old young lady who chose to give him up at birth. Her family supported her decision. Jeff's parents went through the Roman Catholic Services requesting a child. They waited and waited. This is just beautiful how Jeff tells it.

"Five years later, they got a phone call. We have a baby for you. They went to the hospital the day I was born. My dad and I have a song that connects us called Two Less Lonely People from Air Supply. And he said when they handed me to him, I just looked at him and I looked at my mom, and he just knew that there was going to be three less lonely people in the world. That we all were made for each other. And I'm so grateful. I'm grateful to my birth mom and her family for making the right decision. My parents are the most wonderful parents in the world. And I am very blessed and honored that God brought me to them."

Jeff understands the gravity of this situation. A young lady made a courageous choice empowering him to have the life his parents have given him. It's no wonder he loved Landon before he was born and wanted to love him well.

But taking ownership of being a dad is only one of the life-altering choices Jeff has made. Remember he was involved in the rock and roll world and that hadn't changed. When I met him, Landon was about five years old. He talked about Landon all the time, just like he talked about his parents. But his life was on a collision course with destruction. His weight was skyrocketing, and the doctor told him his liver would fail if he didn't stop the drinking. *"I was drinking, nonstop. I was drinking at shows. I was drinking at rehearsal. We would do a song and we would all do a shot; we would all drink a beer. Part of my contract was every time we would go to the studio; the fridge was filled with beer and liquor and all that stuff. That was part of my contract. That's a messed-up thing to have part of the contract."* So, what made the change? Someone else who loved him.

When Jeff was working on his new album *Winds of Emotion*, he hired an orchestra. The guitar player's name was John. This guy was a Christian and kept inviting Jeff to church. Jeff repeatedly turned him down. *"I pretty much had sworn off God."* Finally, just to make him stop, Jeff went with him. He figured he'd go once and then this guy would get off his back. Having no intention to listen Jeff found himself impacted by the music, especially a certain song. *"And I just put my arms on the railing because we were in the balcony first row and I was just lost. Just totally pulled in by this gentleman singing and the music."* Captivated and open, Jeff started listening as the different people spoke. He'd been in church before, but it was never like this. Their words penetrated his heart. *"For the first time in my life I was in a religious place and they were asking what do you need from this message? What do you need to take from it to better your life?"* Jeff was well aware he needed to make a change. He'd come expecting to find form and repetition but got open arms and offers for help instead.

After that service Jeff "*gave John the biggest hug in the world.*" He then sat in his car for almost an hour overcome with emotion and letting the experience sink in. "*I felt God come back to me. And it was the most powerful, amazing feeling in the world.*" Jeff started reaching for freedom from the dark path he was on. He returned to that church and looked for help through his family, motivational books and YouTube. "*There's two vloggers that really helped me focus and bring out the best of myself. One is Roman Atwood. And the other one is Yousef Erakat.*"

Little by little, day by day, Jeff got stronger on the inside until the day he owned his sobriety. "*I was doing a show at Freedom Hill in Sterling Heights, Michigan. I stepped off stage and I had a beer in my hand. I looked at my backup singer, and I handed it to him. And I said, I will never drink again. All the guys started laughing 'Okay, buddy, all right.' And I haven't. I stopped on a dime. I said, I don't need this in my life. I'm happy and proud to say that I'm almost four years sober. I only focus now on being a good father, a great son, and my career.*" Jeff is living the life he dreamed of as a boy.

Jeff told me he always sang. A cousin that babysat him told him how he sang his heart out in the bathtub as young as two-years old. When he was just four years old his parents gave him a piano and Jeff taught himself how to play. They continued to give him instruments and he learned to play them all. "*At one point my whole basement was full of different instruments. And I would go from one to the next, to the next, the next.*"

Playing instruments was something Jeff loved to do, but it got him in trouble with bullies at school. He was different, and they made sure he knew it. When playing football was the cool thing to do, Jeff was singing, writing music and playing instruments. Jeff's parents helped him overcome them by feeding his self-worth and encouraging his gifts. They helped him realize different wasn't bad, it was just different. *"I made it cool. I made it be my thing. I just stepped up and I owned it, to this point, to this day."* Now, Jeff is helping his son overcome bullies in his life. He's doing it with the same unconditional love and support he received from his parents. *"When I told them that I want to be a professional singer, they said we'll do everything in our power to help you reach your dreams. Not many parents do that or say that."*

Jeff and I talked about how some parents have a mold they expect their child to fit into and when they don't, the parent becomes the bully. But when a parent loves and accepts their child empowering their dreams, a child can do amazing things. Jeff is proof of this.

Another gift Jeff was given by his parents is trust. The young lady who gave birth to Jeff had written him a letter. Jeff's parents saved it and gave it to him on his eighteenth birthday. They could have been scared of Jeff's response and withheld it. Instead they took courage allowing him to fully own who he is. In this letter Jeff discovers the origin of his musical talent. *"So here I'm eighteen years old reading a letter from my sixteen-year-old birth mother. And you can tell, it was a 16-year-old writing this. But the craziest part was when she's explaining my birth father. She goes, 'I love to roller skate up to Metro beach and sit on the picnic table and look at the water. And then your birth father comes up with his guitar and sings to me. He has the most beautiful voice you have ever heard.' Isn't that crazy they're musical lovers."* Finding this out didn't cause Jeff to love his parents any less. What it did was make him even more thankful she made the choice she did, and he gets to live the life he has.

Anyone who sees Jeff at one of his shows or follows him online knows how much he loves what he does. *"I get to wake up every day doing what I love to do, and to me that's much more rewarding and much richer than anything money can buy."* He travels around the country doing shows. And now that Landon's older he gets to come along. The joy in Jeff's heart is tangible.

The honor and respect I sensed in Jeff from the beginning is something he owns. He spreads it everywhere he goes. He loves people and wants them to know their value. It doesn't matter who they are, how old or young they are, what color they are, or anything. In fact, Jeff is quite involved in various fundraisers and charity work. He and his mom do many things for St. Jude. But I could hear his heart as he talked to me about Penrickton Center. *"They are a nonprofit that I go and visit and it's just so amazing to see. This is a school for blind children, but they're not only blind. They have another disability. They might be blind with downs. They might be blind with speech impediments. They might be blind with missing limbs. There's a lot of different things going on there. And these people, help these kids grow and better themselves; find what they love and passions that they have. And the most amazing thing I would have to say is that they have a music room. They say music is the gateway for these kids. And that's just unbelievable. That music is just such a beautiful, beautiful thing."*

Find out more about Jeff and what he has to offer in the endnotes.

CHAPTER 13

Owning Your Purpose

For we are God's handiwork, created in Christ Jesus to do good works, which God prepared in advance for us to do.

—Paul

HOW TO BEGIN

The word purpose can sound big and intimidating. It's not uncommon for people to get hung up trying to find their purpose. Been there, done that. It can feel like there's a single huge thing we have to accomplish, but it's playing hide and seek with us. Purpose doesn't have to be just one thing. Purpose simply means to have a reason, or intention to do something. Living an intentional life is living with purpose. We can make intentional choices every day and that's living on purpose. Purpose will often be revealed in the midst of the everyday. So, take a breath, remember you matter. Every. Single. Day. Learning to love, and take ownership of your life, might be the purpose you need for now. Remember the choice is yours.

I dare you to own your purpose, one day at a time, gracefully and intentionally.

OWN THE POSSIBILITIES THAT GIVE HOPE

Jesus looked at them and said, "With man this is impossible, but with God all things are possible."

—Matthew

When pressure is strong against you, and you've been struggling for a while, you feel like giving up. That's when hope is powerful. Hope will arise when you own the possibilities. The drive to quit says there are no possible answers, cures, victories, help or whatever it is you need. The pressure lies. Emotional and mental pressure can be blinding. I endured great pressure the day I first wrote about owning your victory, in the chapter *Owning Your Process*. I'd been going through difficulties for a couple months. Some more serious than others, but just when I thought the trouble stopped, it simply changed form. It went from physical to technical. I sought solutions. I exhausted what I knew. I got partial victory, yet there were things I had no answers for. I was tired. I was frustrated. The pressure was pushing me to give up. I resisted, yet felt so weak. I couldn't see how to overcome. And then it happened.

I remembered what I'd written a few hours before and burst out laughing. Here I was falling under the pressure until those words slapped me out of it.

- I needed to own the victory I couldn't see.
- I needed to believe and own the possibility, despite my lack of vision.
- I needed to own the hope, to keep going.

The mental and emotional pressure was trying to sell me toxic, yet addictive hopelessness. I didn't buy it. As long as I have breath in me, things are possible. The word impossible is a hope stealer. God is famous for making a way where there seems to be nothing but impossibilities. Look at these impossibilities God turned around:

There's a king in the Bible, named Jehoshaphat.[32] He got word two armies were planning to come and annihilate them. They had no way to win in such a battle. That's some alarming news to get. Jehoshaphat took this seemingly hopeless situation to the Lord. God made a way. It sounded crazy. God said to send singers out in front of the army, singing Praise the Lord, His mercy endures forever. Can you imagine being one of those singers? But Jehoshaphat chose to trust God, and do what He said, and those under his authority carried out the plan. The result was the enemy troops got confused and killed each other instead of who they had planned to kill. Jehoshaphat and his people took three days carrying all the spoils the enemy had left. God turned the impossible into profitable.

The Israelites were slaves in Egypt and God sent Moses to bring them out. After a grueling time of plagues and confrontations with the Pharaoh, they were finally allowed to leave. But then Pharaoh changed his mind, and chased after them, catching up to them next to the Red Sea. This massive crowd of men, women, and children were cornered. They had a body of water in front of them, and a powerful angry army behind them. Talk about some fear! But Moses brought this seemingly impossible situation to the Lord. God made a way. It sounded crazy. He told him *"Raise your staff and stretch out your hand over the sea to divide the water so that the Israelites can go through the sea on dry ground."* Can you imagine God telling you to do something like that? But Moses listened, and the sea opened. They not only got across, but the sea closed upon Pharaoh and his armies. God turned the impossible into permanent deliverance.

And let me remind you of Bethany Hamilton's story. Having your arm bitten off by a shark sounds like the end of a surfing career to me. It wasn't to Bethany. Like Jehoshaphat and Moses, she took her seemingly impossible situation to the Lord, and God turned what tried to kill her, into something for her benefit.

God is able to do so much more than we can imagine. Pressing into Him is where we find the possibilities providing hope because it's true *with God all things are possible.*

Own the possibility God will make a way when you feel hopeless.

OWN YOUR STORY: WRITING YOUR STORY CAN CHANGE YOUR LIFE

Owning your story is the bravest thing you will ever do.

—Brené Brown

When I began writing my story, I had no idea how empowering it would be, and how much it would change my life. I was writing because my life had already changed so much. I wanted to help others. But when you look at your story as a story, you look at it differently causing you to see it differently. When you examine what you've been through, for its value to others, you learn things. You risk being vulnerable in an effort to lift others up. You also discover answers to question you didn't know you had.

Finding words to express yourself, and inviting others into your emotions, is an intimate affair. Allowing others access to secret parts of you solidifies what's yours. It's your story. It's not other people's view or opinion. It's how YOU lived it. It's real.

Owning the reality of what you've been through, understanding it might not have been accurate to the circumstances validates your personhood. There's only one you. And sharing your story, fully owning it, is scary, courageous, and empowering. It will change you . . . and that's only the writing part.

Writing is getting what's inside you out onto paper (or screen). When you read what you wrote, you look in a mirror. In the same way we're capable of blurting out words verbally in emotions, we do this in writing as well. As you write, you learn, you change, you alter who you are. Do this *because you matter*. Your story matters.

Then I encourage you to be courageous again. Share your story and your transformation with others. Because they matter. And they have a story to tell also. Writing, sharing, and inspiring others can create a perpetual cycle of healing and wholeness.

Own who you are and who you become through writing your story.

OWN YOUR TEACHABLENESS: THERE'S ALWAYS MORE TO LEARN

Our troubles begin the moment our teachers believe they know it all, and our learners think they are not teachable.

—Israelmore Ayivor

We're familiar with the line *learn something new every day*. Yet it's easy to fall into the mindset that we know everything; or, we know everything we need to know. It's good to own the things we've learned, but there's always more to learn. Having a teachable heart serves us well. This takes humility. No one knows everything except God. We know this, but pride can slip in and mess things up. By owning our teachableness we slam the door on arrogant pride.

Teachableness has a craving to continually learn. We can do this in many ways: books, classes, or online courses. Taking up a new hobby can help us. Because when we submit ourselves to learn something new, we understand we don't know everything. This helps us have a humble heart. Why does this matter? Because pride (the know it all kind) brings destruction; but, humility brings honor. There is a good kind of pride: the self-respect and honor when you've done a job well, overcome an obstacle, or attained a goal. This kind of pride can be humble at the same time. It understands there's more to learn. It owns teachableness and makes room for continuous growth.

Good pride and humility can work together. They celebrate progress and victories along the pathway of learning. Continuing to learn aids growth.

Own your teachableness to become all you were designed to be.

OWN YOUR LIFE AND PURPOSE: WHAT YOU DO AFFECTS OTHERS

"For I know the plans I have for you," declares the Lord, "plans to prosper you and not to harm you, plans to give you hope and a future."

—Jeremiah

Many years ago, I wrote a song called *"What We Do Affects Each Other, Like it or Not."* The song was lame, but the lesson impacted me so much it stuck with me. In this world where we can feel alone, it's important to remember we aren't, and who we are and what we do, matters. This isn't to put any undue stress on us. We aren't in charge of anyone else's life. We aren't powerless either. We're amazing complex beings created in the image of the Almighty God for relationship. We have a purpose. Our lives matter. We can be a force for good on this earth. It can be difficult to grasp if we struggle with a small perception of ourselves, aka as low self-esteem (like we've already talked about). Don't get mired down in buzz words, or the familiar. Instead, remember it's about how you see yourself. If you see yourself as a part of the community, called humanity, you'll see a natural connectedness. If you see yourself as a member of the body of Christ, you'll see another purpose in your connections. Own where you want to be connected.

You have the power for an impact that can cause domino effects. Some large. Some small. When we help others, we also help ourselves. Every person has an inner need for purpose. Many times, people look to others for their purpose. But the power lies within you. It's your life. It's your purpose. God put it there. Don't hand it to a fellow human. That doesn't serve you or them. Don't pawn it off on God either. He didn't make you a puppet or a robot.

Take ownership of your life and live it with complete intention.

KEY POINTS

- Purpose doesn't have to be just one thing. Purpose simply means to have a reason, or intention to do something.
- Hope is powerful. Hope will arise when you own the possibilities.
- Writing, sharing, and inspiring others can create a perpetual cycle of healing and wholeness.
- When we submit ourselves to learn something new, we understand we don't know everything.
- You have the power for an impact that can cause domino effects. Some large. Some small.
- Take ownership of your life and live it with complete intention.

YOU CAN ASK GOD FOR HELP

Thank you, God, that you love me and my life matters. Help me to help others, and to reach for help when I need it myself. Spirit of Grace, help me see purpose in the everyday affairs of life, and not get hung up on some huge vague expectation. Help me see all the good inside of me, nurture it and share it with others.

NOTES

More from the Author

If you loved this book, pick one up for a friend, and leave a review on Amazon. Share the love.

Other Books by Danielle

Emerging With Wings: A True Story of Lies, Pain, And The LOVE that Heals
A Bird Named Payn
Love's Manifesto – free upon request dani@daniellebernock.com

Resources for You

https://www.daniellebernock.com/free-resources/

The Victorious Souls Podcast

Connect on Social Media

https://www.facebook.com/daniellebernock/
https://www.instagram.com/dbernock/
https://twitter.com/DBernock
https://www.pinterest.com/DanielleBernock/
https://www.linkedin.com/in/danielle-bernock-6ab50467/

For Speaking, Coaching, Workshops, and Courses

Visit https://www.daniellebernock.com or email dani@daniellebernock.com

For Bulk Orders

Email dani@daniellebernock.com

Endnotes

CONNECT WITH THE INTERVIEWEES

ANDRE MILLS

Website: https://www.purposestrategics.com/

JACKIE TROTTMAN

Website: https://www.jackietrottmann.com/

Meditations: https://www.jackietrottmann.com/shop/

Amazon Author page: https://www.amazon.com/Jackie-Trottmann/e/B072J812T8?ref=sr_ntt_srch_lnk_1&qid=1557339040&sr=1-1-spell

JEFF CAVATAIO

Website: https://jeffreycavataio.com/

Music: www.jcavmusic.com

JOHN THURMAN

Website: https://johnthurman.net/

MARY O'DONOHUE

Website: https://maryodonohue.com/

Media Savvy Author: https://maryodonohue.com/media-savvy-author/

Mary's book on Amazon: https://www.amazon.com/gp/product/144050377X/ref=dbs_a_def_rwt_bibl_vppi_i0

NANCY BOUWENS

Website: https://www.nancybouwens.com/

NAOMI TROTTO

Website: https://www.salonbellamore.com/

Instagram: https://www.instagram.com/naomitrotto/

RANDY ARWINE

Ministry website: https://ahm4.life/

SYLVIA HUBBARD

Website: https://sylviahubbard.com/

Motown Writers: https://motownwriters.wordpress.com/

Amazon Author page: https://www.amazon.com/Sylvia-Hubbard/e/B002BLN0RG?ref=sr_ntt_srch_lnk_2&qid=1557941090&sr=1-2

TOM SHEA

Email: Tshea58@comcast.net

SCRIPTURE

Chapter 1: Why This Book

"In this world you will have trouble . . ." —John 16:33 NIV

"I am come that they might have life . . ." —John 10:10b

But by the grace of God I am what I am, and . . . —1 Corinthians 15:10a NIV

Chapter 3: Owning Your Choices

. . . do all things through Christ. —Philippians 4:13

. . . more than a conqueror. —Romans 8:37

Greater is He that is in you. —1 John 4:4

Chapter 4: Owning Your Value

The LORD appeared to us in the past . . . —Jeremiah 31:3 NIV

The Lord your God is with you . . . —Zephaniah 3:17 GW

God created mankind in his own image . . . —Genesis 1:27 NIV

For God so loved the world that he gave . . . —John 3:16 NIV

Make a careful exploration of who . . . —Galatians 6:4-5 MSG

Be sure to do what you should, for then . . . —Galatians 6:4 NLT

Chapter 5: Owning Your Courage

There is no fear in love . . . —1 John 4:18 NKJV

Love is patient, love is kind . . . —1 Corinthians 13:4-8 NIV

The second half of the verse. . . —1 John 4:18b

Be made new in your hearts . . . —Ephesians 4:23-24 ERV

...who received the word with all readiness... —Acts 17:11

The Bible tells us Jesus took our sicknesses... —Matthew 8:17

...love covers a multitude of sins. —1 Peter 4:8b NLT

Two are better than one. —Ecclesiastes 4:9-10

"Let's go at once and report this to the royal palace." —2 Kings 7:9b NIV

Chapter 6: Owning Your Mess

He heals the brokenhearted and binds up their wounds. —Psalm 147:3 NIV

"Blessed are those who mourn, for they will be comforted." —Matthew 5:4 NIV

Chapter 7: Owning Your Pain

To everything there is a season... — Ecclesiastes 3:1

My times are in thy hand: deliver me... —Psalm 31:15

Chapter 8: Owning Your Emotions

He has made everything beautiful in its time... —Ecclesiastes 3:11 NIV

As water reflects the face, so one's life reflects the heart. —Proverbs 27:19 NIV

"Everyone who hears these words..." —Matthew 7:24-27 NIV

Peter got down out of the boat, walked... —Matthew 14:29-31 NIV

Suddenly a furious storm came up... —Matthew 8:24-27 NIV

Let us hold unswervingly to the hope... —Hebrews 10:23 NIV

The blood bought right. —Deuteronomy 28:41 NIV and Galatians 3:13

"Let's make a small room on the roof . . ." —2 Kings 4:10 GW

Chapter 9: Owning Your Mind

Wisdom is the principal thing . . . —Proverbs 4:7

Walking down the street, Jesus saw a man . . . —John 9:1-5 MSG

And God is able to bless you abundantly . . . —2 Corinthians 9:8 NIV

Beloved, I wish above all things that . . . —3 John 2

And you shall remember the Lord your God . . . —Deuteronomy 8:18 NKJV

You will be enriched in every way so . . . —2 Corinthians 9:11 NIV

. . . there is no condemnation for me . . . —Romans 8:1 NIV

It is for freedom that Christ has set me free . . . —Galatians 5:1 NIV

The one who is throwing me into confusion . . . —Galatians 5:10 NIV

That kind of persuasion does not come from . . . —Galatians 5:8 NIV

But the fruit of the spirit is love, joy . . . —Galatians 5:22 GW

Chapter 10: Owning Your Grace

Where the Bible says we're saved by grace. —Ephesians 2:8

We love him, because he first loved us. —1 John 4:19

". . . with shoutings, crying 'Grace! Grace!'" —Zechariah 4:7

. . . all things God works for the good . . . —Romans 8:28 NIV

God shall supply all your need according . . . — Philippians 4:19

Each time he said, "My grace is all you need . . ." —2 Corinthians 12:9 NLT

. . . all things through Christ . . . —Philippians 4:13

His anointing has the power to not only . . . —Isaiah 10:27

How He holds it all together with His word. —Hebrews 1:3

God on your side. —Psalm 118:6

God's bigness through worship . . ." —Psalm 34:3

Jesus said – "Come to me you who are weary . . ." —Matthew 11:28

If we believe not, yet he abideth faithful . . . —2 Timothy 2:13

. . . denied knowing Jesus with swearing . . . —Mark 14:66-71 NIV

. . . just as Jesus had predicted. —Matthew 26:33-34 NIV

He remembered . . . —Matthew 16:15-16 NIV

Jesus had not only predicted . . . —Luke 22:31-34 NIV and John 21:15-17

Two are better than one. —Ecclesiastes 4:9-10 NIV

What Jesus said about John the Baptist . . . —Matthew 11:11 NIV

"Look, the Lamb of God . . ." —John 1:29-34 NIV

Where Jesus asked his disciples about their faith —Matthew 8:26 NIV

You are my hiding place; you will protect . . . —Psalm 32:7 NIV

. . . songs of deliverance . . . —Psalm 32:7

. . . when he was running from . . . —2 Samuel 22:1-3 NIV

Chapter 11: Owning Your Process

To everything there is a season, and a . . . —Ecclesiastes 3:1

My times are in thy hand: deliver me from . . . —Psalm 31:15

Now all glory to God, who is able . . . —Ephesians 3:20 NLT

. . . He gives us the victory . . . — 1 Corinthians 15:57 (NIV)

. . . God, who always leads us . . . —2 Corinthians 2:14 (ERV)

"A good man brings good things out of . . ." — Luke 6:45 NIV

To everything there is a season and a . . ." —Ecclesiastes 3:1

. . . the mouth speaks what our heart . . . —Matthew 12:34b NIV

. . . there's no condemnation . . . —Romans 8:1 NIV

. . . you're the righteousness of God in . . . —2 Corinthians 5:21

. . . and God will help you. —Isaiah 41:10 NIV

Death and life are in the power of the tongue. —Proverbs 18:21

Once and for all . . . —1 Peter 3:18 NIV

He became sin . . . —2 Corinthians 5:21NIV

God is not the source of it. —1 Corinthians 14:33 NIV

. . . no condemnation for me who is in Christ . . . —Romans 8:1

It is for freedom that Christ has set me free. —Galatians 5:1

The one who is throwing me into confusion . . . —Galatians 5:10

That kind of persuasion does not come from . . . —Galatians 5:8

. . . fruit of the Spirit is love, joy, peace . . . —Galatians 8:22-23

. . . our knowledge is partial and . . . —1 Corinthians 13:9 NLT

Consider it pure joy, my brothers and . . . —James 1:2-4 NIV

When we have the greater one in us . . . —1 John 4:4 NIV

. . . let the Spirit renew your thoughts . . . —Ephesians 4:23 NLT

". . . as a grain of mustard seed . . ." —Matthew 17:20

But blessed is the man who trusts . . . —Jeremiah 17:7-8 TLB

Chapter 12: Owning Your Wholeness

"Now this is eternal life: that they know . . ." —John 17:3 NIV

"The wind blows wherever it pleases. You . . ." —John 3:8 NIV

"It is the Spirit who gives life . . ." —John 6:63 NIV

For God so loved . . . me . . . you . . . —John 3:16

. . . who is joined to the Lord is . . . —1 Corinthians 6:17 NLT

. . . these are written, that ye might believe . . . —John 20:31

. . . in hope that he believed . . . —Romans 4:18 NIV

Where Abraham was fully persuaded. —Romans 4:21 NIV

. . . what Abraham was hoping . . . —Hebrews 11:1 GNT

. . . to hear the promise of God . . . —Romans 10:17

. . . great love the Father has lavished . . . —1 John 3:1a NIV

. . . the Bible as the fall. —Genesis 3

. . . a little lower than Himself crowned with glory. —Psalm 8:5

For you know that it was not with . . . —1 Peter 1:18-19 NIV

. . . all have sinned, and come short of the . . . —Romans 3:23

"I gave them the same glory you gave . . ." —John 17:22 GNT

"I pray not only for them . . ." —John 17:20-24 GNT

. . . made me the righteousness of God . . . —2 Corinthians 5:21

. . . kingdom where we are called royal . . . —1 Peter 2:9 NIV

. . . a new covenant . . . —Hebrews 8:6 NIV

. . . His ministry is superior . . . —Hebrews 8:6 NIV

"I will not leave you comfortless . . ." —John 14:18

Chapter 13: Owning Your Purpose

For we are God's handiwork . . . —Ephesians 2:10 NIV

Jesus looked at them and said . . . —Matthew 19:26 NIV

"Raise your staff and stretch out your . . ." —Exodus 14:16 NIV

God is able to do so much more . . . —Ephesians 3:20 NIV

. . . with God all things are possible . . . —Matthew 19:26 NIV

For I know the plans I have for you . . . —Jeremiah 29:11 NIV

References

Chapter 1: Why This Book

1. "How Do Butterflies/moths Spread Their Wings After Emerging?" Reiman Gardens, Iowa State University, Ames, Iowa, Butterfly House.
http://www.reimangardens.com/butterfly/butterfliesmoths-spread-wings-emerging/

"Rearing Adults" Butterfly Fun Facts Butterflyfunfacts.com

Chapter 2: Why Ownership

2. Definitions.Net

3. Strong's Concordance New Testament word #1438

Chapter 3: Owning Your Choices

4. "Tyler Perry's Traumatic Childhood." Oprah.com.
http://www.oprah.com/oprahshow/Tyler-Perry-Speaks-Out-About-Being-Molested-and-the-Aftermath.

"11 Tyler Perry on Oprah Discussing Abuse." YouTube. March 28, 2018. https://www.youtube.com/watch?v=f0ifsqTJ56E.
"I Know I've Been Changed." Wikipedia, the Free Encyclopedia. Last modified February 19, 2018.

5. "Young Surfer Who Lost an Arm in a Shark Attack Refuses to Give Up | The Oprah Winfrey Show | OWN." YouTube. July 2, 2014. https://www.youtube.com/watch?v=ffgxXjGPrT4.

"Bethany Hamilton Childhood Clips and Photos." HistoryvsHollywood.com.
http://www.historyvshollywood.com/video/bethany-hamilton-childhood-clips-and-photos/.

Bethany Hamilton. https://bethanyhamilton.com/.

Chapter 4: Owning Your Value

6. "LOVE'S MANIFESTO." Connecting People to The LOVE That Heals https://www.daniellebernock.com/loves-manifesto/.

Chapter 5: Owning Your Courage

7 "A Quote from Emerging with Wings." Goodreads | Meet Your Next Favorite Book. https://www.goodreads.com/quotes/7003849-trauma-is-personal-it-does-not-disappear-if-it-is.

8. "Bible Gateway Passage: Genesis 1-3 - New International Version." Bible Gateway.
https://www.biblegateway.com/passage/?search=Genesis+1-3&version=NIV.

9. "Bible Gateway Passage: 2 Kings 7 - New International Version." Bible Gateway.
https://www.biblegateway.com/passage/?search=2+kings+7&version=NIV.

10. "Who Said the Same Sun Melts the Wax and Hardens the Clay." Answers.com.
https://www.answers.com/Q/Who_said_the_same_sun_melts_the_wax_and_hardens_the_clay.

Chapter 6: Owning Your Mess

11. "How Building Implosions Work." HowStuffWorks. Last modified June 26, 2001.
https://science.howstuffworks.com/engineering/structural/building-implosion.htm.

12. Bernock, Danielle. Emerging with Wings: A True Story of Lies, Pain, and the LOVE That Heals. 4F Media, 2014. Chapter 11 bRokEn Mirrors

13. Bernock, Danielle. Emerging with Wings: A True Story of Lies, Pain, and the LOVE That Heals. 4F Media, 2014. Chapter 11 bRokEn Mirrors

Chapter 7: Owning Your Pain

14. Updated/revised from original story A Bird Named Payn 4F Media (October 27, 2017)

Chapter 8: Owning Your Emotions

15. Beck, Julie. "New Research Says There Are Only Four Emotions." The Atlantic. Last modified February 4, 2014. http://www.theatlantic.com/health/archive/2014/02/new-research-says-there-are-only-four-emotions/283560/.

16. "Emotion Wheel / Wheel of Emotions by Robert Plutchik." ToolsHero. Last modified July 18, 2018. https://www.toolshero.com/psychology/personal-happiness/emotion-wheel-robert-plutchik/.

17. "How Many Emotions Are There and What Are They?" Online Therapy & Free Counseling, Someone To Talk To | 7 Cups. Last modified June 18, 2018. http://www.7cups.com/qa-managing-emotions-4/how-many-emotions-are-there-and-what-are-they-101/.

18. "The Hazards to Aircraft in Thunderstorms." Pilot Resources Aviation Resources Aviation Weather Flight Training for General Aviation. http://www.pilotfriend.com/av_weather/meteo/thnder.htm.

19. "Safe Flying in Unsafe Weather'€Š'€Š" Rotor & Wing International. Last modified July 1, 2011. https://www.rotorandwing.com/2011/07/01/safe-flying-in-unsafe-weatheraesaes/.

20. "Bloomberg." Bloomberg - Are You a Robot? http://www.bloomberg.com/news/articles/2014-12-30/how-bad-weather-can-affect-aircraft-and-what-can-be-done-qa.

21. "How Dangerous is Flying in a Storm?" The Telegraph. http://www.telegraph.co.uk/travel/travelnews/travel-truths/11342494/How-dangerous-is-flying-in-high-winds.html.

22. Ibid.

23. "The Plane and The Wind." The Physics Classroom. http://www.physicsclassroom.com/mmedia/vectors/plane.cfm.

24. "Safe Flying" (n 19)

Chapter 11: Owning Your Process

25. Bible Times Nursery Rhymes by Emily Hunter Outskirts Press (May 15, 2013)

26. Bernock, Danielle. Emerging with Wings: A True Story of Lies, Pain, and the LOVE That Heals. 4F Media, 2014. Chapter 12 Puzzle Pieces

Chapter 12: Owning Your Wholeness

27. Interdependence - Dictionary Definition. (n.d.). Retrieved from https://www.vocabulary.com/dictionary/interdependence

28. The Bible itself says—Galatians 4:24-5:1 NLT and James 1:27 GNT

29. Strong's Concordance Old Testament word #430

30. Bernock, Danielle. Emerging with Wings: A True Story of Lies, Pain, and the LOVE That Heals. 4F Media, 2014. Chapter 14 Getting Wings

31. Bernock, Danielle. Emerging with Wings: A True Story of Lies, Pain, and the LOVE That Heals. 4F Media, 2014. Chapter 14 Getting Wings

Chapter 13: Owning Your Purpose

32. Jehoshaphat—2 Chronicles 20 NIV

www.ingramcontent.com/pod-product-compliance
Lightning Source LLC
Chambersburg PA
CBHW030432010526
44118CB00011B/602